MUTUAL FUND RULES

PREVIOUS BOOKS BY MICHAEL D. SHEIMO

Bond Market Rules (1999)
Stock Market Rules (2nd edition) (1999)
The International Encyclopedia of the Stock Market (1998)
Cashing In on the Dow (1997)
The Stock Selector System (1994)
Stock Market Rules (paperback) (1993)
Stock Market Rules · (1991)
Dow Theory Redux (1989)

MUTUAL FUND RULES

50 Essential Axioms
to Explain and Examine
Mutual Fund Investing

MICHAEL D. SHEIMO

McGraw-Hill

New York San Francisco Washington, D.C. Auckland Bogotá
Caracas Lisbon London Madrid Mexico City Milan
Montreal New Delhi San Juan Singapore
Sydney Tokyo Toronto

Library of Congress Cataloging-in-Publication Data

Sheimo, Michael D.
    Mutual fund rules: 50 essential axioms to explain and examine
mutual fund investing / by Michael D. Sheimo.
      p. cm.
    ISBN 0-07-135025-x
    1. Mutual funds—Handbooks, manuals, etc. I. Title.
HG4530.S49 1999
332.63'27—dc21   99-32835
                                             CIP

McGraw-Hill

*A Division of The **McGraw·Hill** Companies*

1 2 3 4 5 6 7 8 9 0 DOC/DOC 9 0 9 8 7 6 5 4 3 2 1 0 9

ISBN 0-07-135025-X

The sponsoring editor for this book was Kelli Christiansen, the editing supervisor was John M. Morriss, and the production supervisor was Elizabeth J. Strange. It was set in Palatino per the IPROF design specs by Joanne Morbit and Michele Pridmore of the Hightstown McGraw-Hill Desktop Publishing Unit.

McGraw-Hill books are available at special discounts to use as premiums and sales promotions, or for use in corporate training programs. For more information, please write to the Director of Special Sales, McGraw-Hill, 11 West 19th Street, New York, NY 10011. Or contact your local bookstore.

This publication is designed to provide accurate and authoritative information in regard to the subject matter covered. It is sold with the understanding that the publisher is not engaged in rendering legal, accounting or other professional service. If legal advice or other expert assistance is required, the services of a competent professional person should be sought.
From a Declaration of Principles Jointly Adopted by a Committee of the American Bar Association and a Committed of Publishers and Associations.

 This book is printed on recycled, acid-free paper containing a minimum of 50% recycled de-inked paper.

Once more for Linda, with mutual love.

CONTENTS

A penny saved is a penny earned.

Benjamin Franklin

However, a penny invested carefully can become worth much more. Most people want their money to be well invested, but do not want to have investing become like a second job. Investing in mutual funds can be a low-maintenance, effective, and reasonably safe approach, whether you are investing retirement money, savings, or inheritance money.

According to the Investment Company Institute's latest survey of the mutual fund industry, the combined assets of the nation's mutual funds were $5.622 trillion in February 1999. Mutual funds have come a long way since the first one, Massachusetts Investors Trust, started in 1924.

RULES

The "rules" concept of using axioms to organize an investing book began with *Stock Market Rules* back in the year 1990. The 50-chapter book simply explained the meaning behind old Wall Street sayings. It examined how individual investors could learn from and make use of the information presented. The book was still selling well in 1999, updated and revised as a second edition. The same concept was used for *Bond Market Rules*, also published in 1999, and it became only logical to follow with this book for mutual fund investing.

AXIOMS

Just as Ben Franklin's wise sayings taught short, useful lessons in life, the axioms in this book present short, useful lessons for investing. Whether it's the concept of "Pay Yourself First" in Chapter 1,

"Look Out for Ponzi Scams" in Chapter 3, or "Invest According to Objectives" in Chapter 18, the concise, clear chapters leave the reader with useful information.

THE BEST FUND

We all want the best fund, although it might not be the best for us. Top performers one year aren't necessarily in the same rank the following year. Things change, and top performance depends on a number of factors, including risk. The better approach is to find the best fund for you. Which fund has acceptable parameters that will fit your objectives, needs, and life stage? It might be a top performer now and then, but that's not necessarily the most important feature. Knowing and understanding the risk involved is oftentimes more important than performance.

DIVERSIFICATION

Understanding specific details of diversification and how risk can be examined is important. Many people assume that all mutual funds are diversified. Yes, they are, but some are much more diversified than others. Whereas greater diversification might lead to lower performance in the short term, it can also mean greater safety for the long run.

LONG TERM

The stock market fluctuates—it goes up, it goes down—but over the long term, it goes up. That is why you should consider mutual funds only with a long-term perspective. *Long term* with mutual funds usually means a minimum of 5 years. Therefore, it is essential that a mutual fund investment be the best fund for you.

MORE SOPHISTICATED

Mutual fund investing used to be a simple matter. You'd pick out a fund and buy it. Originally, the funds were all quite similar. That was before. Now, mutual funds have become highly specialized, with varying levels of risk and reward combinations. Even funds that might look the same at first glance are quite different on closer examination. One growth fund might put 25 percent of the assets into emerging markets, while another stays with only mid-sized-to-large U.S. companies. One index mutual fund will match the Standard & Poor's 500 Index, while another tries to beat the Russell 2000 Index, and yet another describes itself as "enhanced." So what's the difference in risk? Find out in Chapter 47, "Index Funds Follow the Market."

INVEST THE PENNIES

Earn those pennies, save those pennies, and invest them with care. It would be easy to make an argument saying that virtually every individual's investment portfolio should include some mutual fund allocation. Whether you decide to put all or some of your assets into a group of funds or a single fund, this book will show you how and help you understand why.

CHAPTER 1

Pay Yourself First

The first rule of investing, "Get Some Money."
The second rule of investing, "Don't lose it."

Anon.

In order to get some money an investor either inherits it or works for it. Although the people who inherit money are often blessed, most people are not so fortunate; most have to work for the money. And of the people who have to work for it, some earn a lot and some much less. But no matter how much or how little money a person is able to earn, it is always important to pay yourself first. It might be a significant amount of money or a modest amount, but the pattern needs to be established as soon as possible.

LIVE WITHIN YOUR MEANS?

No. Don't live within your means. Live *below* your means. Living within your means is spending every penny earned, and that's never a good habit to develop. It might be good for the federal government, but not for individuals and families. Although living within one's means is better than living beyond one's means, it's not much better.

If necessary, take a second job in order to be able to pay yourself first and have enough money left over for the basics and pleasantries. This can be especially effective when one is young and healthy and has the energy to work two or more jobs.

CALCULATE AND SET SPENDING PRIORITIES

Write Down Monthly Income

On a blank sheet of paper, write your monthly income. If your income is different every month, state it as an average or choose a lowest amount.

Pay Yourself First

Make a guesstimate about how many dollars you think you will be able to pay yourself each month. Whether it's $500, $1,000, or only $40 a month doesn't matter. What matters is the saving habit.

Use Windfalls as a Savings Bonus

Many individuals can't wait to spend that small or large inheritance, bonus from work, or insurance settlement. It's a new VCR, stereo, or television set, and poof, the money's spent and forgotten. If current debts are not burdensome, it might be better to borrow the money and make time payments. Use the windfall as an investment bonus. Of course, that means don't spend that income tax return—invest it where some savings growth can occur.

List Essential and Flexible Expenses

List monthly expenses, e.g., food, housing, utilities, transportation, loan payments, and insurance (if paid twice a year, divide by 6). Then list flexible costs, such as credit card payments.

List Nonessential Expenses

List elective spending like restaurants, movies, or other forms of entertainment.

Calculate the Core Living Expense

Adding up the expenses will provide a dollar amount needed for every month. It is the core amount of money needed for survival.

Subtract that amount from your monthly income. The hope is there will be some extra money. If the number is negative, either some trimming or another source of income is necessary.

RECALCULATE HOW MUCH TO PAY YOURSELF

You might be able to pay yourself more than you believed initially. Be careful not to set the amount so high that it becomes impossible. It can easily lead to borrowing from savings for necessities, and that can quickly destroy the savings.

WHAT ABOUT SETTING A BUDGET?

Sure, setting a budget is OK if the budget is followed regularly. But following a budget is something many people have trouble doing. A budget that is forgotten or ignored as soon as it is created becomes an exercise in futility. In many family and individual situations, a carefully planned weekly grocery list will usually save more money than a detailed budget.

PAY YOURSELF AUTOMATICALLY

Whether it's by having a specific amount of money automatically transferred to savings, transferred to a retirement program at work, or sent to a mutual fund every month, paying yourself automatically is usually painless. It also tends to remove the temptation to spend any extra cash.

Pay yourself first. It can be surprising how quickly the money piles up for investment. It is difficult for most people to save money. America once was a frugal nation, but that frugality has been replaced by deficit spending. The availability of credit, unfavorable taxation on savings, and a general change in attitude have all made us a debtor nation, from the government to the individual citizens.

SAVING IS ESSENTIAL FOR RETIREMENT

Saving and investing in the next millennium will become essential for retirement. The social security system could easily go the way of the horse and buggy or the railroads. It seems like the more Congress fixes social security, the worse it becomes. Either it is too big a problem, or it will continue to be bandied about until it's too late to accomplish meaningful reform. One of the main problems is that politicians look at social security as a political statement rather than an economic reality. Moving steadily away from debt and toward prudent investing could be the only strategy offering people a real opportunity for retirement.

CHAPTER 2

Let the Fund Do the Work

The world has become a place of specialization. Sadly, there's not much room anymore for the renaissance man or woman, who is an expert on many subjects. That special individual who could manage the household expenses, figure the taxes, keep track of the income, build the savings, and do the investing has become a rarity. Everyone has too much work to do. Either the constantly increasing demands of employment or the additional commitments to their growing families are bankrupting people of time. Even leisure activities are becoming increasingly structured.

LOOK TO EXPERTS

Many individuals intend to learn about investing, so that they can improve on their certificate of deposit returns, but they have trouble finding the time. Consequently, they turn to the "experts," the professional portfolio managers of mutual funds. As one can imagine, the number of people opening mutual fund accounts has grown tremendously in the past decade.

GROWTH OF MUTUAL FUNDS FOR THE TWENTY-YEAR PERIOD 1977–1997

1977

The Investment Company Institute[1] figures for 1977 show that 427 mutual fund companies had 8,515,100 mutual fund accounts with net assets of $45 billion.

1987

Ten years later in 1987, with 1,776 companies reporting, there were 36,855,000 accounts with net assets of $453.8 billion. That's quadruple the number of accounts with more than ten times the money. But that's not all.

1997

In 1997, 5,765 mutual fund companies reported that the number of accounts had grown to 135,689,000 (Figure 2-1) with net assets of $3,430.8 billion. That is nearly a 16-fold increase in the number of accounts in 20 years (Figure 2-2). Net assets in these 1997 accounts were $3,430.8 billion, just over 76 times more than in 1977.

There's nothing like a good stock market to get investors into mutual funds. Much of the growth in the number of accounts has occurred since 1994. The number of accounts is not the same as number of investors, since many investors have more than one mutual fund account. Some people invest in more than one fund to extend diversification, and others select funds of different types.

Net Asset Increase

Although the increase in the number of accounts is significant, it is rather small when compared with the increase in net assets. The net assets of a mutual fund represent the fund's true value, after any charges or fees have been deducted. The net asset value is what an investor would receive if the shares were sold. If you look at the total net asset value of a mutual fund or group of funds, keep in

---

1. *Mutual Fund Fact Book*, May 1998, Investment Company Institute, http://www.ici.org.

FIGURE 2-1

Mutual Fund Growth, Number of Accounts, 1990–1997.

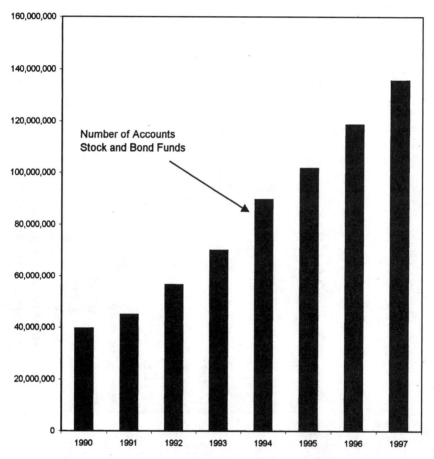

mind that it includes money invested, as well as market appreciation due to increasing prices (Figure 2-2).

DIVERSIFICATION AND PERFORMANCE

Investors have learned that diversification is an important safety
consideration, and mutual funds are diversified. Most realize
they are at risk if the stock market declines, but they will likely
participate when the market advances. They let the mutual fund

FIGURE 2-2

Mutual Fund Growth, Dollar Net Assets, 1977–1997.

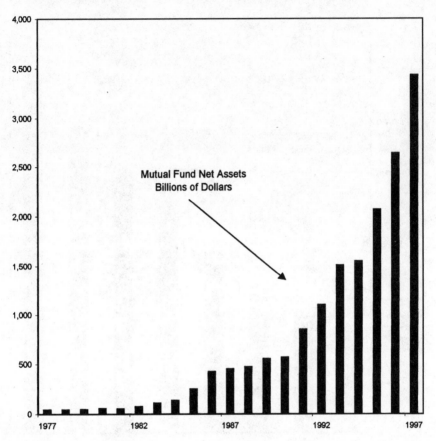

do the work. Some watch the activities of their mutual fund and compare performance with other funds. Others seldom look at the investment and periodically buy more shares. They believe that their work is done once the fund is selected.

LOW-MAINTENANCE INVESTING

Many individuals look at mutual funds as low-maintenance investing. Funds are the "buy-and-forget" investment. People put their money down in the hope that it will grow at a rate considerably higher than inflation for the next several years. If they get really lucky, they might be able to retire with a good income.

Although these investors should watch their fund performance, the low-maintenance approach isn't totally incorrect. Most mutual funds are designed for the long-term-growth investor. They are not an investment for the short-term, more speculative investment objective. Investors should intend to stay with a mutual fund at least 5 years.

Compare performance, but make certain the comparison is fair. It's not fair to compare the results of a conservative growth and income fund with the results of an aggressive growth fund. In a strong market, the aggressive growth fund should show the higher performance, but it also has higher risk.

Most of the work related to mutual fund investing is selecting a fund that has investment objectives with which an investor can be comfortable. An acceptable risk level, reasonable performance, with an equitable cost—these are the areas an investor needs to analyze. When the fund is selected, let the portfolio manager do the work.

CHAPTER 3

Look Out for Ponzi Scams

A billion dollars, according to the Federal Trade Commission, is how much money individuals lose to investment fraud every year. Perpetrators of fraud often run a particular scam for a short time, quickly spend or hide the money, and then close down before they can be detected. Later, they open under another name and sell another investment scam. Some work alone, others operate as a team, fleecing an unsuspecting public.

IT'S GUARANTEED

Fraudulent investment scammers are articulate and resourceful. They might say that they have high-level financial connections and are privy to inside information. They'll guarantee the investment or buy it back after a certain time. They know how to serve up phony statistics, misrepresent the significance of a current event, or stress the unique quality of their offering to deter many from verifying their story.

PARTLY GREED AND PARTLY NOT

Part of falling for a scam is greed, but there is more. Many people have a deep belief that they will get lucky if a special opportunity comes their way, and they are willing to put their money on the line. These people are especially vulnerable to "guaranteed" investments and frequently will not ask for further details. They invest thousands of dollars, which are quickly paid out to earlier investors to keep the scam operating. If they are fortunate enough to be early in the scam, they receive high returns on their money, usually for a short time. If returns are paid out, it is to keep the original investors happy and have them recommend the opportunity to others. Thus, the scam snowballs, growing larger with each new investor until people start saying no. Eventually it becomes impossible to pay out the high returns. The perpetrators of the scam shut down the operation and move on to new investors.

IT'S A CLASSIC PONZI SCAM

The name *Ponzi* came from Charles Ponzi, who moved to Montreal from Italy. Later he moved to Boston. While working as a clerk, he became interested in a mailing he received describing postal coupons and the favorable exchange rate with Spain. Ponzi believed he could establish a system to profit from the currency exchange rates for the International Postal Reply Coupons (IPRCs). He calculated that he could pay a small amount for the coupons in a country with weak currency and redeem them at a profit in the United States where the currency was strong.

A Different SEC

After establishing a company on the second floor of a bank building in 1919, called the Securities and Exchange Company (the U.S. government regulatory SEC wouldn't exist until 1930), he established a pyramid scheme in December and mailed out prospectuses. The information offered a 50 percent investment return in 45 days and 100 percent in 90 days. By the end of June 1920 (6 months) he was reported to be receiving $500,000 a day and paying out $200,000 daily.

Lines around the Block

People flocked by the thousands to invest their money. A line would usually form down the stairs and around the block. Ponzi had to hire no fewer than 16 clerks to count and sort the money, which was then stored in wastebaskets and closets.

Eventually the pyramid of cash fell apart. Newspapers began to point out that there were not enough postal coupons in existence to pay the returns Ponzi was still offering. When the district attorney closed Mr. Ponzi's operation at the end of July, more than 30,000 people had invested $9,582,591 during the 8 months of operation. The average size of investment was $319, small even for 1920; but for some, it represented their total life savings.

Just Deserts

Charles Ponzi became bankrupt and served 7 years in federal prison. It was learned that Ponzi only engaged in token postal coupon transactions totaling about $30 during the first weeks of the scam. After serving prison time he was deported to Italy, at his own request. He died, essentially penniless, in Brazil, where he worked in an Italian air line office. Although it is believed he invented the scheme, he did not; just the same, the name *Ponzi* became attached to the scam, also known as a pyramid scheme.[1]

BEFORE INVESTING, FIND OUT

With any investment, it's better to get information before investing than after. Before investing in a mutual fund, get answers to the following questions, as recommended by the North American Securities Administrators Association:[2]

What are the mutual fund's goals and investment strategies?

What are the fees and other costs, and how do they compare with comparable funds?

How are the costs determined?

What is the fund's performance and management history?

---

1. Sherm Robbins, based on information from "Ponzi—Explained," *Your Business Bulletin Board*, Special Report, October 1995, http://pages.prodigy.com/Computing/ybcp/.
2. Bulletin for Older Investors, by the American Association of Retired Persons, the Consumer Federation of America, and the North American Securities Administrators Association, April 1997, http://www.nasaa.org/investoredu/investoralerts/bloldinv.html.

How does it compare with similar funds?

Are derivatives used in the fund?

If derivatives are used, are they used for hedging (lower risk) or speculating (higher risk)?

Who makes investment decisions for the fund?

Whom can you call for more information?

Obtaining answers to questions like these can give an investor a solid understanding of any mutual fund. The information might not totally insulate an investor from fraud or fraudulent activities, but it can help one better understand what a specific fund is trying to accomplish and how.

CHAPTER 4

Follow the Yield Curve

Virtually all investment securities are influenced by interest rates. As interest rates rise significantly, stocks, bonds, and unit trusts, as well as mutual funds of stocks and bonds, decline in price. Higher interest rates mean tighter money, and it becomes more difficult and expensive for companies to operate. Revenues, earnings, and growth are slower. Consequently stock prices increase slowly or begin to decline. Existing bond prices decline in order to match current yields pushed up by the higher interest rates.

FUND PRICES DECLINE

Since stock prices tend to move as a group, mutual funds of stock will follow a market decline. Just as bond prices are adjusted downward to compensate for higher yields, bond mutual fund and unit trust prices will also go lower with higher interest rates.

INFLATION OR PREVENTION OF INFLATION

Higher interest rates can be caused by an assault of inflationary trends, or rates can be temporarily raised by the Federal Reserve Bank in order to stop a trend. Using higher interest rates to stop inflation is rather like using fire to fight fire. A small increase now prevents big inflation later. A small interest rate hike is intended to keep the economy from overheating or overproducing, thereby helping to prevent a recession.

EFFECTS OF LOWER INTEREST RATES

As interest rates drop, the prices of securities increase. Stock prices increase in anticipation of increased corporate earnings. When interest rates go down, the cost of doing business is lowered and earnings increase. Bond prices increase to adjust bond current yields to the new lower interest rates.

TREASURY BOND YIELD CURVE

Although any bond with varying maturity lengths has a yield curve depending on maturity dates, when the term *yield curve* is discussed, it usually refers to U.S. Treasury bills, notes, and bonds.[1] Effectively, these three are all bonds, debt securities issued by the U.S. federal government. Bills have short maturities, notes are medium-term maturities, and the longer maturities are bonds.

WHAT IT IS

The yield curve is a constantly changing graph line showing interest rate levels on different maturities of these Treasury securities.

ANALYSES

Some financial analysts observe the yield curve movements for signals of strength and weakness in the economy. Such analysis is difficult and time consuming, and frequently arrives at incorrect conclusions. Such conclusions were possibly the source of the old joke about economists predicting nine out of the last five recessions.

NORMAL, STEEP, FLAT, OR INVERTED

Four words often used to describe the yield curve are *normal, steep, inverted,* and *flat.* To many, there is no such thing as "normal" in the

---

1. Sometimes corporate bond yields are added for comparison.

markets or the economy. Each day, week, month, and year has qualities that make it unique. In this book, however, we recognize the existence of a normal yield curve.

Normal Yield Curve

The yield curve for November 1994 was a normal yield curve (Figure 4-1). From the figure, you can see that the short-term rates are the lowest, and they get gradually higher, with only a small dip at the end. A normal yield curve is believed to be a sign of a healthy, steady

FIGURE 4-1

Normal Yield Curve, November 1994.

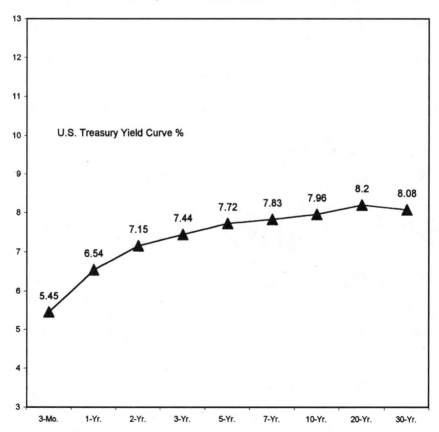

economy. The growth is slow but consistent. Stock and bond markets tend to be steady likewise. It must be stressed that the yield curve is not a predictor but rather an indicator. Sudden bear markets can appear even when the yield curve appears relatively normal.

Steep Yield Curve

At times, the yield curve can be quite steep, suggesting that change could be coming to the economy. The difference between short- and long-term yields is often about 3 percent, but when it increases to 4 or 5 percent, it obviously creates a steeper curve (Figure 4-2). Such

FIGURE 4-2

Steep Yield Curve, October 1992.

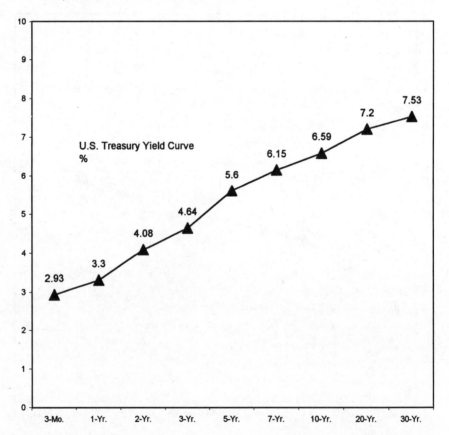

a curve suggests long-term bondholders believe the economy will improve in the near future. Steep yield curves frequently appear after recessions, as the economy stabilizes and begins expansion.

After the slight recession of 1991, the yield curve became steep in the following April. The difference between the 3-month and the 30-year bond became 4.12 percent. A year earlier the difference was 2.38 percent between the short and long. Just 6 months earlier it was only a 2.79 percent difference, and 3 months earlier the gap was 3.67 percent. The gap grew until October of that year when it reached a steep 4.6 percent. Short-term rates were forced down to make low-cost money available to stimulate business expansion. The strategy worked and business expanded.

Flat Yield Curve

On its way to inverting, the yield curve can become flattened. Although a flat curve is considered an early warning of inversion, at times the curve works its way back to normal without becoming inverted. It is not unusual for a flat curve to be followed by an economic recession. With the lowest yield at 7.9 percent and the highest at 8.03 percent (Figure 4-3), one could say that all yields for October 1989 were virtually 8 percent. The curve is about as flat as it can get.

Inverted Yield Curve

When short-term money pays a higher rate than long term, it signals the opposite of expansion. This is a time of contraction. It's time to reign in the oxen and circle the wagons because the economy is overproducing and possibly heading for a recession. Interest rates are pushed up to make it more expensive to borrow money for business expansion. If action is taken soon enough, it can lessen the effects of a recession or even prevent its occurrence. The inversion is caused by bond buyers buying up the longer bonds, anticipating a drop in interest rates. The ensuing lower interest rates will be necessary to stimulate the economy out of recession. As investors buy the long bonds, the demand pushes prices higher and yields lower.

August 1981 (Figure 4-4) shows a yield curve where the 1-year bond is 2.55 percent higher than the 30-year bond. Although the shorter bond has a significantly higher yield, its attractiveness

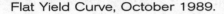

FIGURE 4-3

Flat Yield Curve, October 1989.

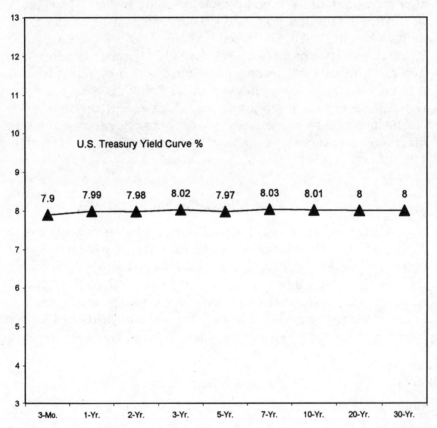

is lower because it will only be for a year. It's interesting how, for the 1-year and longer-term bonds, the rates drop lower as each maturity is extended. Even the short-term 3-month T-bills are higher than the 10-year and later bonds.

INDICATOR

Although the yield curve can be used as an indicator of possible changes in the economy, as well as the stock and bond markets, like most indicators it is not precise. Although it can be helpful to keep an eye on the yield curve as an indicator, it should be used in conjunction with other indicators and information, including economic news, as well as what's happening in the stock market.

INVESTMENT SELECTION

The data can also be directly used for investment selection. If an investor believes interest rates are stable or likely to go lower, it would be prudent to lock in the highest yield on the 20-year bond or long-term bond unit trust. It would also be a good time to buy into a growth and income stock mutual fund. If a fixed-income investor believes that interest rates are likely to rise, it might be prudent to invest in something shorter term.

FIGURE 4-4

Inverted Yield Curve, August 1981.

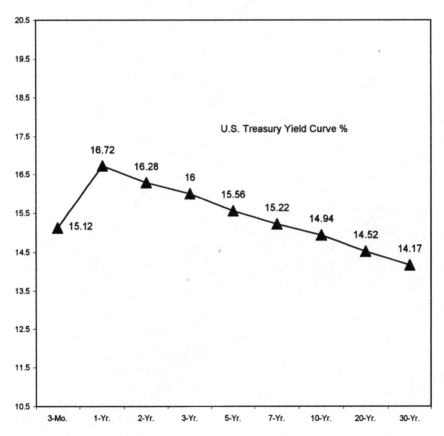

CHAPTER 5

Ask Questions, Get Answers

Once the decision has been made to invest in a mutual fund, it's time to contact a representative at a brokerage firm or bank, who will mail literature out to the investor. Time can be saved by giving the representative a clear picture of investment goals and concerns about risk. Ask what funds are available that could closely match the goals, and have two or three prospectuses mailed out. Also, ask for statements of additional information and any sales literature that might be available.

Then sit down at the table and search for answers.

FIND ANSWERS

1. According to the Prospectus, What Is the Fund's Objective?

What type of fund is described? The fund type defines the objectives; the style describes the methods used to pursue the objective.

2. What Is the Fund's Style?

How does the fund invest money to achieve its objective? What's the strategy or style? Does the fund buy stocks in blue-chip companies

or small, speculative companies? Does the fund use derivatives for
hedging (conservative) or yield enhancement (riskier)?

3. What Risks Are Involved with the Fund?

The answer to this one might take some digging into the information, but some statement of risk should appear in the prospectus.
The new push for "plain English" should help the search. Look for
anything in the literature that might appear to increase the risk. Is
the fund manager new? Is the fund allowed to invest in securities
outside the main strategy for higher yields? How has the fund performed in down markets?

   Market risk is the most familiar to investors. When the market
goes down, they expect a mutual fund, invested in similar securities, to also drop. But there can be other risks with mutual funds.

Interest Rate Risk
The value of the securities declines as interest rates rise. Bond
prices decline as interest rates rise. Likewise the share value of a
bond mutual fund will decline.

Credit Risk
Risk of nonpayment (default) rises with higher-yielding bonds.
Although this can be a reason to buy a fund of bonds, a bond in
default will affect the fund negatively.

Liquidity Risk
Are the shares easily bought and sold? Liquidity in the markets is
the ease with which one can buy and sell securities. Although the
vast majority of mutual funds should be easy to buy and sell, one
should always ask about liquidity with every investment.

Currency Risk
Mutual funds involved with international investing can lose value
due to fluctuations in currency exchange rates.

Political Risk
Political risk can be encountered with some foreign (non-U.S.)
investing where value can be lost due to unfavorable political or
regulatory changes within a country's investments.

4. What Fees and Management Expenses Are Involved?

These should be clearly stated on a table in the front of the prospectus. If there is any confusion, ask the representative to explain or call the mutual fund company.

5. Who Manages the Fund?

What firm acts as investment adviser? Who is the portfolio manager? How long has the manager been in charge of the fund? What is the manager's background?

6. How Are Shares of the Fund Purchased?

Are shares purchased directly from the fund? Do they have to be obtained through a broker? What about future purchases? Is an automatic purchase plan available? What is the smallest purchase possible? Can dividends, capital gains, and other distributions be automatically reinvested?

7. How Can the Shares Be Sold?

Are there any minimums on the sell? Is there any cost to sell? Are there any special requirements to sell? When will the money be available? By law, a U.S. mutual fund must be ready to buy back mutual fund shares on any business day. Normal pricing is based on the net asset value at the end of the trading day.

8. How Are Distributions Made and Taxed?

Mutual fund distributions can be dividends or capital gains made from the sale of securities. Most funds allow you to automatically reinvest the distributions or have them paid out to the investor. Distributions are usually taxable events even if they are reinvested. Although tax-exempt interest is paid from municipal funds, capital gains distributions are taxable. Capital gains on the sale of shares should also be considered when selling mutual fund shares.

9. What Services Are Available to the Investor?

Does the fund allow "switches" from one fund to another in the same family of funds? If so, what is the charge and what restrictions are there on switches. How often will information be sent out regarding the account? Does the fund have automatic information and transaction features? Are there automatic investment and withdrawal plans, retirement plan features, or check writing?

CLEAR UNDERSTANDING OF THE FUND

By the time these questions are answered, the investor should have a good understanding of a mutual fund candidate. Comparing one fund with a couple of others can bring out enough differences to help in the decision-making process. Finding answers to these questions might also generate other areas of concern to discuss with the fund representative or with a broker.

CHAPTER 6

Mutual Funds Have Less Risk

Risk is anything that might cause an investor to lose money. Essentially, there are four main types of risk:

1. Investment risk
2. Market risk
3. Credit risk
4. Inflation risk

INVESTMENT RISK

All investments have risk in one form or another. To obtain higher returns, an investor must be willing to assume greater risk. Conversely, if one chooses to minimize risk, it is necessary to accept lower returns. Although greater rewards usually have higher risk, it does not necessarily follow that higher risk brings greater rewards.

Investment risk is when an investor buys XYZ Company stock at $50 a share and it drops to $10 a share. It's buying IBM at $150 a share and having it drop to $75 a share. It's buying an Internet stock at $15 a share and having it go to zero.

Mutual funds provide protection from investment risk. The protection comes from being diversified into the securities of several different issuers. It's not just the stock of IBM or XYZ

Company, but rather a professionally selected basket of stocks from several companies. If one company goes bad or has hard times, the investor has protection if the other securities in the fund do well. If all or many of the securities in a mutual fund have problems, the value of the fund drops accordingly.

MARKET RISK

A bear market or a severe market correction can bring the price of a mutual fund down. Many individuals look at market drops as buying opportunities, where the mutual fund is available at sale prices. Others become nervous and are ready to sell. Except for the crash of 1929, which continued to 1933 and drove many companies out of business, most buyers in down markets have done better than sellers.

Common stocks have provided a return of 11 percent on average over the last 60 years, but that means almost nothing compared with the last 5 years, when the returns have been considerably higher. The conservative Dow Industrial Average has averaged a 29 percent increase each of the 5 years, and the Standard & Poor's 500 Index has shown a nearly 34 percent average annual increase. So much for that measly 11 percent 60-year average.

A look at the Dow Industrial Average shows how things change in a 60-year time frame (Figure 6-1). The Dow prior to 1954 shows little relationship to the 1954–1982 segment, and that segment is dramatically different from the 1982–1999 time frame.

Recent History

The past year or recent 5 years are usually more meaningful than earlier years (Figure 6-2). Business and economic changes happen quickly. Analyzing too long a period can make things appear better or worse than they look in the present.

Stock prices tend to move as a group. If a leading average like the Dow Industrials or a leading index like the Standard & Poor's 500 has dropped several points, most stock mutual fund prices will also be down. In the chart in Figure 6-2, an investor buying a stock mutual fund when the Dow is at point A would see the net asset value of that fund drop when the Dow dropped at point B.

FIGURE 6-1

Changing Market, Dow Industrials, 1939–1999.

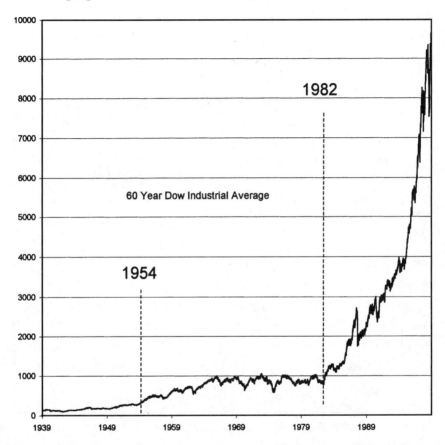

The only reliable mutual fund protection from market risk is the type of securities in the fund. Aggressive growth funds will tend to drop more than conservative growth or growth and income funds. Some funds take portfolio insurance measures, but the effectiveness is debatable.

CREDIT RISK

In addition to interest rate risk, bonds and bond funds are subject to credit risk. Credit risk is the possibility that the issuer of

FIGURE 6-2

Market Risk, Dow Industrials, 1994–1999.

an individual bond will default (fail to make timely payments of principal and interest). Lower-quality bonds have a greater risk of default than higher-quality bonds and generally offer higher yields to compensate investors for assuming the extra risk. Government bonds offer the lowest yields but carry the highest credit ratings and, thus, have the lowest risk of default. However, government bond prices have significant changes as interest rates change (market risk). If interest rates increase, bond prices decline.

INFLATION RISK

Inflation is an increase in the price level of goods and services. It reduces the "real" return over a number of years. Investing needs to have a return higher than inflation in order to provide future income.

Historically, common stock prices have significantly outpaced inflation. Bonds have stayed slightly ahead of inflation, and short-term money market investments have barely kept up with inflation. Money hidden away and not invested declines by the amount of inflation.

INVESTING HAS RISK

All investing has varying degrees of investment risk, market risk, credit risk, and inflation risk. These risks cannot be completely avoided, but they can be moderated by investing in mutual funds. Risk can be further moderated by selecting the fund with a strategy that matches an individual's objective and risk tolerance level.

CHAPTER 7

Use the Rule of 72 to Double[1]

So…if you're saving for a specific purpose, like your child's education, once you have figured out an estimate of how much money you'll need, how much does your current investment have to grow to be there? Or possibly you simply want to know how much growth each year you need from your mutual fund purchase for it to double in 5 or 10 years.

A quick, easy method of calculation is to use the rule of 72, which essentially calculates the number of years any investment will take to double at a given rate. Don't rush out and buy a new computer to do the math. In fact, many times even a calculator is unnecessary.

FORMULA FOR THE RULE OF 72

The rule of 72 allows you to calculate the approximate number of years required for your investment to double with varying growth rates Maybe you want to know when your portfolio will double if it grows annually at 20 percent. Simply divide 72 (a magic number) by 20 (percent growth rate) and round off to the nearest number. You know right away that 72 divided by 20 is 3.6, rounded up to the whole number 4. It will take approximately 4 years for your portfolio to double at a 20 percent annual return.

---

1. This chapter is taken from Michael D. Sheimo, *Stock Market Rules* (2d ed.), McGraw-Hill, New York, 1999.

OK, YOU WANT LESS RISK

What if you "only" earn 15 percent a year, because you think the 20 percent is too risky? Decide for yourself. Again, divide 72 by 15 and round the answer to the nearest number. It comes to 4.8. Round up, and the answer is it would take 5 years to double. So what do you get in money market savings, 3 percent? OK—72 divided by 3—the money will double in 24 years.

HOW MANY YEARS TO DOUBLE?

The number of years to double equals the number 72 divided by the percent growth rate (rounded), as shown below:

Percent growth rates	5	6	7	8	9	10	11	12	20	25
Years to double	14	12	10	9	8	7	7	6	4	3

PRECISION NOT REQUIRED

Of course, the results with the rule of 72 aren't precise. However, they are close enough to count and can be quickly and simply calculated. The formula is intended to be a fast and easy way of calculating.

PERIODICALLY RECALCULATE

It's a good idea to recalculate the doubling time annually, based on the return for the previous year. In the stock market, returns tend to continually change, and the investor might get 20 percent one year and 5 percent the next. The recalculation will help the individual stay on track to pay for the college education or attain any other goal.

CHAPTER 8

All Mutual Funds Aren't the Same

It seems like every month a new type of mutual fund emerges. Mutual funds tend to be categorized by a generalization of their objective. There are three general categories: equity funds (stock), income or fixed-income funds (bond funds), and money market funds. These are further divided into general subgroups, which can then be divided into even more specific specialties.

I. STOCK FUNDS

Aggressive Growth Funds

Aggressive growth funds aim to maximize capital gains. The managers don't care about current income in the form of dividends. What they want to see is rapid price growth. These are the managers looking for the next Microsoft or IBM, *before* the stock price rises. The funds may leverage their assets by borrowing money (margin loans), and may trade in stock options.

If the market is going up, these funds will often benefit the most. Conversely, aggressive growth funds are hardest hit when the market turns bearish. The high volatility of these funds makes them inappropriate for the more conservative, risk-aversive investors.

Growth Funds

Growth funds are similar to aggressive growth funds, but usually don't trade stock options or use margin money to trade. Current income from dividends is not part of the strategy. They tend to invest in the common stock of well-established companies. Growth funds often surpass the S&P 500 Index during bull markets, but tend to perform below average during bear markets. These funds can also have considerable volatility, making them inappropriate as the only investment for risk-averse investors.

Growth and Income Funds

Growth and income funds are specialists in blue-chip, usually dividend-paying, stocks. They often invest in utilities, Dow Industrial Average stocks, and others. They attempt to maximize dividend income while generating capital gains. The funds are suitable for conservative investments in the stock market.

Precious Metal Funds

Precious metal funds invest in gold, silver, and platinum. They seek to achieve capital gains by increases in the prices of the metals

International Funds

International funds hold primarily foreign securities, seeking capital gains by price increases. Most or all of the securities in these funds are of companies located outside the United States. Although they can be quite profitable in a favorable market, individual funds can be too volatile for the average investor as a sole investment.

Global Equity Funds

These funds seek growth in the value of their common stock investments. They invest in stocks throughout the world, including the United States. The inclusion of U.S. stock is to give the fund additional stability in the sometimes volatile world markets.

Income-Equity Funds

Income-equity funds focus on dividend income from common stock. They also enjoy the capital gains that often accompany investment in common and preferred stocks. The funds tend to select stocks with good dividend payment records and are often of interest to conservative investors.

II. BOND AND INCOME FUNDS

Flexible Portfolio Funds

The flexible funds allow the managers to anticipate and respond to changing market conditions. They can invest in stocks, bonds, or money market securities depending on the current market conditions.

Balanced Funds

Balanced funds normally have preservation of capital as a priority. They pay current income and seek long-term growth. The portfolios are usually a mix of bonds, preferred stock, and common stock with dividends.

Income-Mixed Funds

The usual objective is a high level of income. Income-mixed funds invest in income-generating securities, including both stock and bonds.

Income-Bond Funds

With a mix of corporate and government bonds, these funds seek a high level of current income.

U.S. Government Income Funds

These funds, for current income, invest in a variety of government securities, such as Treasury bonds, federally guaranteed mortgage-backed securities, and other government notes. Some of these funds can also invest in derivatives either as a hedge or for yield enhancement purposes.

GNMA (Ginnie Mae) Funds

GNMA funds look for a high level of current income. Although the majority of their investments are in GNMAs, some will also invest in other government securities.

Global Bond Funds

Seeking a high level of current income, global bond funds invest in the debt securities of companies and governments around the world, including the United States.

Corporate Bond Funds

Most of the assets are invested in corporate bonds for high current income. Remaining assets tend to be invested in U.S. Treasury bonds or other federal agency debt securities.

High-Yield Bond Funds

With higher risk than other corporate funds, these portfolios seek a very high yield. The majority of the funds' assets are invested in corporate bonds that have a lower credit rating.

National Municipal Bond Funds, Long Term

To generate income not taxable by the federal government, these funds invest in the municipal bonds of several states. They are usually taxable at the state level.

State Municipal Bond Funds, Long Term

The fund portfolio is invested in the municipal bonds of one specific state. The yield is tax-exempt at both the federal and state level for the residents of the state whose bonds are in the fund.

III. MONEY MARKET FUNDS

Taxable Money Market Funds

These funds work to keep the net asset value stable. They invest in short-term, high-grade, investment-quality securities in the money market. By investing in short-term Treasury bills, certificates of deposit with large banks, and commercial paper, they keep the maturity at 90 days or less.

Tax-Exempt Money Market Funds, National

Short-term income from municipal securities nationwide is placed into the portfolio. The interest is tax-exempt at the federal level.

Tax-Exempt Money Market Funds, State

Short-term income from municipal securities of a specific state makes up the investment portfolio. The interest is both federal and state tax-exempt.

CHECK THE PROSPECTUS

These are most of the general classifications of mutual funds. Many of them can be further subdivided into more specific fund objectives. Other subdivisions by industry or other sector are also available. Although the category comes from the fund's objective, it is a general statement. Details that are more specific can be found in the prospectus and statement of additional information.

CHAPTER 9

The Highest-Performing Fund Can Be Dangerous

We have become a high-performance group of people. We want the best whenever possible. Second place isn't good enough; only first place will do. The problem with looking at high performance with investments is that it is virtually always accompanied by higher risk. If the stock or bond market performance has been favorable, the more speculative mutual funds will be the high-performing funds. Higher risk can come from bonds being actively traded or from derivatives.

BE SUSPICIOUS OF HIGH YIELDS

In the mid-1990s, much of the mutual fund fraud encountered by industry regulators was from yield-hungry portfolio managers in a declining interest rate market. The fraud impacted governments, like the Orange County, California, debacle; some banks; and a few mutual funds.

Concerned that investors would remove their money if interest rates dropped too low, some fund managers turned to derivatives as a way to stabilize or increase the yield. Derivatives can be used as a hedge against temporary changes in interest rates. Hedging is a conservative strategy. But the derivatives weren't being used as a hedge. The portfolio managers were speculating on interest rates dropping further. The speculation allowed them to pay higher than normal yields from their mutual funds. Investors remained happy and more importantly stayed with the funds.

As interest rates dropped, managers made money on the derivatives. The gains were added to the funds' yield. But as time passed and rates went even lower, more and more capital became necessary to repeat the performance. Money that had been in conservative, short- and medium-term government securities was converted to cash and invested in highly leveraged (borrowed money), speculative derivatives. As long as interest rates didn't go up, the funds did well. When interest rates moved up, the funds lost millions. This was essentially what happened to a mutual fund managed by Piper Capital Management, Inc., a firm in Minneapolis.

PIPER'S #1 RATED FUND

Piper Capital Management not only managed the Piper Jaffray Institutional Government Income Portfolio (the fund). It also served as the investment adviser for the fund. According to an Associated Press article from July 1998, investors lost nearly $140 million in the fund. The fund claimed to invest in short-term (low price volatility) government securities. Investors bought into the fund convinced it was a low-risk alternative to bank certificates of deposit. Like many such funds, it was allowed to invest in derivatives, usually as a hedge against changes in interest rates. Apparently the fund started as an institutional investor fund and later opened to individuals.

> The Piper Jaffray Institutional Government Income Portfolio was introduced in 1988, with an investment objective of "high current income consistent with the preservation of capital." Initially, the fund consisted almost exclusively of U.S. Treasury notes and government agency mortgage pass-through securities.[1]

According to the NASD, the original fund consisted of U.S. Treasury notes and government agency mortgage pass-through securities. In 1991, apparently this changed as the fund invested in interest rate–sensitive mortgage-backed derivatives. A combina-

---

1. "NASD Fines Piper Jaffray Inc. $1.25 Million for Inadequate Disclosures and Improper Sales Practices," NASD Regulation, Inc., 1997.

tion of these and other derivatives, combined with the use of margin leverage (borrowed money), raised the return potential, but also greatly increased risk.

As of September 1993, as much as 51 percent of the market value of the portfolio was in derivatives, instead of U.S. Treasury notes. The borrowed money exceeded 33 percent of the investment portfolio.

Between 1991 and 1993, the fund was consistently rated as the top-performing fund for short-term government funds by a national rating service, running as much as 5 percent higher than its nearest competition. The year-end of March 1993 showed a total return of 21.7 percent, while the average for similar government funds (noted in the fund's sales literature) was a modest 9.1 percent. Although it's easy to become hooked on a yield like that, most prudent investors would become very nervous. It's more than too high; something had to be wrong.

A look at the yields on 1-year Treasury notes (Figure 9-1) shows how incredible the high yield appeared. Keep in mind, the fund's stated objective was "high current income consistent with the preservation of capital." The 1-year Treasury note would have been consistent with that clear objective, but there's no way it would have paid anything near 21.7 percent.

The exceptional performance of the fund came between points A and B on the chart in Figure 9-1. The fund was originally designed for institutional investors, professionals who should have known that such an unusually high yield meant the fund's risk had to be considerably greater than stated. However, when high yields are coming in, it's not easy for either professionals or individuals to ask difficult questions. Most will hang on and hope for the best.

The greatest threat to the Institutional Government Income Portfolio was higher interest rates, like the line that looks like a wall beginning in February 1994 (point C). Interest rates on the 1-year note more than doubled from 3.5 percent in January to more than 7 percent at the end of the year.

WAS IT FRAUD?

According to the SEC and NASD, fraud was involved, and specific charges were issued. However, the fund itself was not fraudulent;

FIGURE 9-1

One-Year U.S. Treasury Note Yields, 1990–1994.

neither was it a scam. The investment company did not set out to take money away from investors.

The actions of the portfolio manager and others were likely motivated by their belief in the importance of high performance over anything else. Too much performance and not enough discipline for safety, however, can get individual or professional investors into expensive trouble. When preservation of capital is part of a fund's stated objective, it must be adhered to implicitly. When the yields are excessively high, either it's time to find out what the fund is doing or it's time to get out.

THINGS HAVE CHANGED

Since the collapse of Piper Jaffray's fund, things have changed to prevent its costly recurrence. Individuals as well as the company paid a heavy price to fix the problems and make things right with investors.

HIGHER YIELD MEANS HIGHER RISK

High performance normally has a cost, and that cost is higher risk. When selecting an investment for a high return, the investor needs to know what risks are involved. The only way to find out is to read the literature and ask questions.

CHAPTER 10

Determine the Cost of Investing

There are two main types of mutual fund costs: (1) "loads" charged when an investor buys or sells fund shares and (2) expenses charged to the investor for the fund's operation. The impact of these costs can be important. First, however, here are some details of the costs for mutual fund investing.

FRONT-END LOAD

This is a commission or sales charge paid by the investor for buying mutual fund shares. Front-end loads usually are between 4 and 8.5 percent. Loads are also charged for reinvesting dividends in additional shares. A *low-load* fund is a fund that charges 1 to 3 percent of the amount invested. A *no-load* fund does not have any front-end sales charges.

BACK-END LOAD

A back-end load is a charge incurred at the time the investor sells (redeems) the fund shares. The load may be levied as a percentage of the amount sold, or it may be a flat rate. Back-end loads are sometimes referred to as *redemption* or *exit fees.*

A deferred sales charge can impose a 5 to 6 percent charge against the redemption amount on withdrawals made from a fund in the first year. The percentage is normally decreased at a rate of 1 percent per year over a period of 5 to 6 years. For example, in the fourth year as a shareholder, a deferred sales charge that started at 6 percent could decline to 3 percent.

OPERATING EXPENSES

Operating expenses are the costs of operating a mutual fund, including the advisory fees for the investment manager and expenses for fund administrative services. General practice is to state this as an annual percentage of a fund's average net assets (it's called an *expense ratio*). Such costs can range from under 0.25 percent to more than 2 percent of a fund's net assets. It is not unusual, especially with new mutual funds, for the sponsor to temporarily suspend the management fee. This improves the fund's current yield and performance and is a benefit that draws investors to the fund. Suspension of the fee is temporary, and investors should be aware of this when comparing fund yields.

12B-1 PLAN

The 12b-1 charges distribution-related expenses directly against fund assets. "12b-1" refers to the 1980 U.S. Securities and Exchange Commission rule that allows the fees to be charged. A fund is required to include a 12b-1 charge in its stated expense ratio.

EXPENSE RATIOS

Mutual funds are like any other business. They have costs for administrative expenses, and to exist as a company they have to show a profit. An efficient fund will have lower expenses than less efficient funds. Larger mutual funds do business in great volume and can take advantage of an economy of scale. They should have lower expense charges per share.

How to Calculate

Expense ratios can be calculated by dividing annual expenses by average net assets. Fund expenses typically include adviser's fees, legal and accounting fees, and 12b-1 fees, but not commissions, interest on loans, or income taxes. Expense ratios over 2 percent are considered excessive. Funds that consistently perform poorly might have high expense ratios. However, a mutual fund that allows investors in with a low initial minimum investment can also have a higher ratio. The Wiesenberger Investment Companies Service provides this and other types of information about mutual funds. Table 10-1 shows some examples of expense ratios.

DETERMINING MUTUAL FUND COSTS

What's an easy way to learn if a fund is charging a load, redemption fee, or 12b-1 plan fee? Look at the mutual fund listings in a newspaper. Newspaper tables should carry two "prices" for mutual funds—a selling price (NAV) and a buying price [maximum offering price (MOP) or public offering price (POP)]. A mutual fund sell price, or NAV, is its daily closing share price, and it is the amount per share a selling investor receives.

A fund's buy price (MOP or POP) is the amount an investor would pay per share, including any sales charges. To calculate a

TABLE 10-1

Expense Ratio Examples

Type of Mutual Fund Expense Ratio	Ratio, %
Aggressive growth	1.15
Growth and income	1.03
Balanced	0.96
Stock income	1.20
Income (flexible)	1.05
International	1.35
Metals	1.32
Sector	1.35
Government	1.02
Technology	1.27
Other	1.51
All mutual funds	1.15

fund's sales charge, subtract the sell price from the buy price, and then divide by the buy price. Multiplying the result times 100 will state it as a percent. For example, a fund with a $15.00 sell price and a $15.80 buy price has a 5 percent load. ($15.80 − $15.00 = $0.80 ÷ $15.00 = ~ 0.05 × 100 = 5%.)

MUTUAL FUND COSTS

The Securities and Exchange Commission enacted rules in 1988 requiring mutual funds to disclose all fees and expenses in a table near the front of their prospectuses. The SEC requires the "fee table" to include all expenses paid directly or indirectly by shareholders. A fund must also show the cumulative expenses (expressed in dollars) paid on a $1,000 investment at the end of 1-, 3-, 5-, and 10-year periods, assuming a 5 percent annual return.

An example prospectus fee table, shown in Table 10-2, indicates the fees and expenses assessed by three mutual funds.

TABLE 10-2

Shareholder Fee Table

Fees (Directly from the Amount Invested)	Class A	Class B	Class C
Maximum sales charge (load) imposed on purchases (stated as a percentage of offering price)	5.50%	0	0
Maximum deferred sales charge (load) (stated as a percentage of original purchase price or redemption proceeds, whichever is less)	0[1]	5.00%	1.00%
Annual fund operating expenses (Deducted from Fund Assets)	**Class A**	**Class B**	**Class C**
Management fees	0.63%	0.63%	0.63%
Distribution and/or service (12b-1) fees	0.25	1.00	1.00
Other expenses	0.18	0.32	0.32
Total annual fund operating expenses	1.06	1.95	1.95

1. If you buy $1,000,000 or more of Class A shares and redeem the shares within 18 months from the date of purchase, you may pay a 1 percent contingent deferred sales charge (CDSC) at the time of redemption.

Because of 12b-1 fees, long-term shareholders in the fund may pay more than the maximum permitted initial sales charge.

EXPENSE EXAMPLE

The example presented in Table 10-3 is intended to help you compare the costs of investing in different classes of the fund. The example assumes the following:

There is an investment of $10,000 in the fund for the time periods indicated.

All the shares are redeemed at the end of each period.

There is a 5 percent return for each year.

The operating expenses are constant.

Actual returns and costs may be higher or lower.

ALWAYS FEES

Are fees important to investing? Yes, but fees should never be the primary or only consideration when making an investment. Investing money prudently in a mutual fund that shows a

TABLE 10-3

Comparing Investment Costs

Expenses Paid if Redeemed

	1 Year	3 Years	5 Years	10 Years
Class A	$652	$869	$1,103	$1,773
Class B	698	912	1,252	2,044
Class C	298	612	1,052	2,275

Expenses Paid if Not Redeemed

	1 Year	3 Years	5 Years	10 Years
Class A	$652	$869	$1,103	$1,773
Class B	198	612	1,052	2,044
Class C	198	612	1,052	2,275

respectable record of accomplishment and fits the investor's objectives is most important. There are always fees or charges for investing. Even banks charge a fee. The fee is effectively the difference between interest paid on certificates of deposit (and other interest-bearing accounts) and the amount of interest charged on bank loans. Like risk, fees or charges cannot be totally avoided, but careful selection can minimize the impact.

Invest According to Life Stage

Invest according to life stage, needs, and risk tolerance. Of the three, life stage is the only universal, being a direct reference to current age (see Table 11-1). When planning an investment strategy, several age brackets can be used, but it's usually best to keep things simple.

Obviously, as you can see from the table, life-stage periods are primarily based on age. Although many individuals enter the workforce earlier, most start at about age 20. Individuals can afford to take more risk in their early twenties. This is based on the concept that they still have time to recover from losing investments. In regard to taking risks, an investor at this stage should still be prudent, but since retirement is still a long way off, being more aggressive with investing is an acceptable strategy.

Everyone has different comfort levels of risk acceptance. Each person needs to decide how much risk is comfortable in the early

TABLE 11-1

Life-Stage Periods

Age 20 to 40	Aggressive
Age 40 to 50	Moderately aggressive to conservative
Age 50 to retirement	Conservative
Retirement	Most conservative

years. Investing for most at this stage, especially in the early years, will be in some kind of retirement plan. It might be a 401K plan at work or an IRA plan. Retirement plans should tend toward the conservative when considering risk. Higher levels of risk can be considered for investments outside the basic retirement plan.

Investment Asset Mixes

Age 20 to 40—Aggressive

	Income	Growth and Income	Growth	Speculation
Risk	Low	Moderate	Moderate to high	Higher
Assets	5%	20%	50%	25%

At this early stage, it's debatable if any money needs to be invested in straight income; however, this could also be an investor's "emergency fund" money. Investing in high-quality corporate or government bonds also moderates the risk of the rest of the investment portfolio.

Age 40 to 50—Moderately Aggressive to Conservative

	Income	Growth and Income	Growth	Speculation
Risk	Low	Moderate	Moderate to high	Higher
Assets	10%	35%	50%	5%

At this point, it's time to back away from heavy speculation and slightly moderate the investment portfolio. Also, the amount of money in each category is greater than in the first phase. Obviously, an investor could be even more conservative and shift assets into the "Income" and the "Growth and Income" categories.

Age 50 to Retirement—Conservative

	Income	Growth and Income	Growth	Speculation
Risk	Low	Moderate	Moderate to high	Higher
Assets	30%	50%	20%	0%

This is a good time to become quite conservative. The assets have been accumulating for the past 30 years, and it's time to protect them. Investors with a higher risk tolerance can be a little heavier into the growth category, but it's not the age to take big investment risks.

Retirement—Most Conservative

	Income	Growth and Income	Growth	Speculation
Risk	Low	Moderate	Moderate to high	Higher
Assets	70%	30%	0%	0%

Select carefully and don't worry about the market anymore. Here is the time to be the most conservative with investments. Capital preservation leads the way to reliable income. Growth and income are about as speculative as necessary during a period of low interest rates. Income, steady income, is the route to go. It's not time to take a lot of risk, unless one has an excess of assets.

NO ONE FORMULA

The important thing to remember is that there are no formulas cut in stone. The examples here are just that; they are not the only strategy. Risk tolerance or risk acceptance with money is a very personal thing. Each investor must decide on an acceptable level at every age. Acceptance of risk is usually based on experience and fear. Most people follow a route of greatest comfort.

The examples presented here offer a starting point to the individual investor. They can be adapted to fit individual expectations and concerns.

CHAPTER 12

Keep Accurate Records, Always

Record keeping can be an important investment. Records of trades, confirmation slips, and monthly statements can provide information that can be worth extra dollars. At tax time nothing can be more frustrating than trying to find records of transactions for verifying dividends and capital gains or losses. According to the Internal Revenue Service, one of the biggest problems individual investors have is establishing a cost basis for investment purchases.

The cost basis is the amount paid for an investment. When the investment is sold, the cost basis is subtracted from the sell price to determine the capital gains. The tax liability is calculated on the capital gains portion of the investment.

CERTIFICATES HELD

One of the biggest mistakes made by investors is having a certificate delivered and placing it in a safe-deposit box, with no other transaction records. Years later, the investor will wonder what the cost of the investment was at the time of purchase.

The confirmation notice of the buy should be clipped to a certificate when it is stored. This will prevent endless headaches when the stock is sold and it's time to calculate the capital gains.

IRS SIMPLIFIES

The IRS has an easy method of figuring the cost basis when the owner is unable to do so for a stock. The entire proceeds from the sale are considered a capital gain and taxed accordingly. Such action could become costly, especially after 20 or 30 years.

IMPORTANT DOCUMENTS

Investment certificates that are sent out to the buyer are very important documents. They are similar to titles or property deeds. Although they can be replaced if lost, destroyed, or stolen, it takes time. Significant losses can occur while the owner is waiting for the new certificates. Time is lost while a stop is placed on the old certificates and records are searched to ascertain whether the certificates have been previously sold.

MONTHLY STATEMENTS

Monthly brokerage account statements are also important records and should be kept for a reasonable length of time. In some situations, "reasonable" means forever. The information can be helpful in tracking down possible errors or figuring out the details of transactions. Eventually, certificates will be eliminated and all investment securities will be held in book entry format only. Many stock exchanges around the world have already taken this action. It could make confirmations and statements even more important than they are now.

GAINS AND DIVIDENDS

Dividend and capital gains payments from mutual funds are taxable events. The details appear on statements. They are taxable even if automatically reinvested in the funds. Therefore the information is important. Also, if automatically reinvested, the cost basis will be different every time the new purchase is made.

If a bond mutual fund is paying out interest only, the payments are taxed as interest income and not as capital gains. Thus it is not necessary to establish a cost basis. Although interest from tax-exempt funds is not taxed, it still has to be reported. Any capital gains from a tax-exempt fund are taxable income.

AUTOMATIC INVESTMENT AND WITHDRAWAL

Many funds have automatic investment programs where a set dollar amount is transferred from an investor's bank account to the mutual fund. Each of these transfers is a new purchase and can have a new cost basis.

On the other end, mutual funds can set up an automatic withdrawal program, where the investor receives a monthly check. When shares are sold to make these payments, the sell price will have to be compared with a cost basis for tax purposes. Good records become essential for these calculations.

KEEP IT ORGANIZED

An organized system for keeping track of transaction records and certificates can save the investor time and money. Records need to be kept in a safe place—in a safe-deposit box, safe, or special file cabinet. The cost of having an accountant or lawyer sort out the details can be astronomical. Accurate and clear record keeping is an essential part of the mutual fund investment process.

CHAPTER 13

Watch the Consumer Price Index

The consumer price index (CPI) is essentially the official indicator of inflation. Basic inflation is defined as an increase in prices. The CPI measures the change in the price of a "shopping basket" of consumer goods for a country on a monthly basis. The *core* CPI refers to the change in prices of consumer goods except food and energy, since their prices are highly volatile. The core CPI is believed to be the accurate measure of inflation.

A case in point: On May 14, 1999, the Dow made a 211-point correction when it was announced that the core CPI was up 0.4 percent for the previous month. An increase of 0.2 percent had been expected. The surprise increase showed how sensitive the stock market is to inflation.

CPI CALCULATION

An index is a tool to simplify the measurement of movements in a numerical series. Most of the specific CPI indexes have a 1982–1984 reference base. An average index level (representing the average price level) is set for the 36-month period for 1982, 1983, and 1984—equal to 100. Changes are measured in relation to that figure. An index of 110 means there has been a 10 percent increase in price since the base period. An index of 90 would indicate a 10 percent decrease from the 100-base period.[1]

ADJUSTED OR UNADJUSTED

Data on the consumer price index are available in either seasonally adjusted or unadjusted versions. To observe the escalation of inflation, the unadjusted data are recommended as a more accurate view.

CPI AND 10-YEAR TREASURY BOND YIELDS

To compare the CPI with something familiar, Figure 13-1 shows the growth of the CPI in relation to the 10-year bond yields from 1968 to 1998 (through October). Keeping in mind the base of 100 for the 1982–1984 time period, the index is calculated back to 1968.

Notice the acceleration of the curve in the "inflationary spiral" of the 1960s to early 1980s. Inflation peaked in 1980, by rising 13.5 percent for the year.[2] Yields on Treasury bonds peaked the following November with the 10-year yield at 15.32 percent. Clearly, inflation was proving to be difficult to control.

WHAT ABOUT NOW?

A comparison of a period of high inflation to a period of low inflation shows interest rates can be low and inflation relatively under control at the same time. Figure 13-2 shows the 10-year yield dropping from 6.91 to 4.53 percent, while inflation did not appear to accelerate. The CPI rose 9.3 points in the 1996–1998 period, while the 1979–1981 period experienced a CPI increase of 25.6 points.

---

1. Based on information from the Bureau of Labor Statistics Frequently Asked Questions Internet page, 1998, http://stats.bls.gov/cpifaq.htm.
2. *Source: Three Lessons for Monetary Policy,* remarks by Thomas M. Hoenig, President, Federal Reserve Bank of Kansas City, Kansas City, Missouri, Fed Correspondents Association, New York, April 22, 1998, http://www.kc.frb.org/spch&bio/hoenig49.htm.

FIGURE 13-1

Inflation, Consumer Price Index, and 10-Year Bond Yields, 1968–1998.

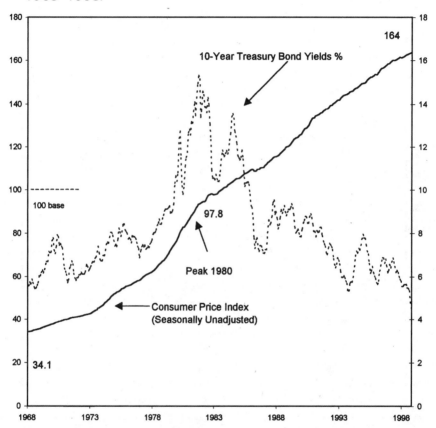

AN INDICATOR

The CPI is an indicator of inflation in the economy. By following its progress, the individual bond investor can develop some understanding of where interest rates are heading. If there is a sudden interest rate increase, is it a preemptive strike on the part of the Fed to halt inflation? Will the money supply be tightened to slow an overheating economy? News reports relating to such increases usually examine the situation extensively and can give the investor good insights into what might happen next.

FIGURE 13-2

Inflation, Consumer Price Index, and 10-Year Yield,
1996–1998.

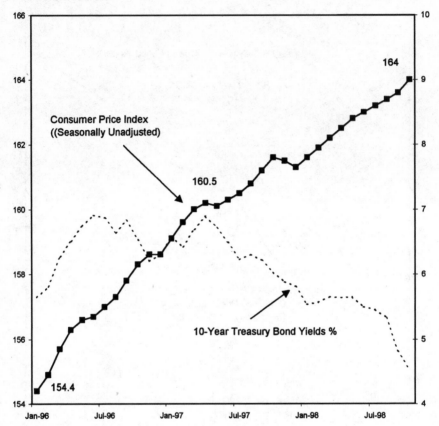

CHAPTER 14

Know the Difference between Deposits and Investments

According to Arthur Levitt, chairman of the U.S. Securities and Exchange Commission, more than 35 million households now invest in mutual funds.[1] That represents one in three American families. Mutual fund assets total more than $4.9 trillion, exceeding insured commercial bank deposits, now at $2.4 trillion.

STRONG MARKET, NEED, AND EASY ACCESS

The 1990s have seen the strongest bull market in history. Although the market hesitated from time to time, there seemed to be no end on the upside. This strong market has pulled investors into the market like never before.

Banks now sell mutual funds, thereby extending their offerings of financial services. Although this is believed to be good for individual investors, some confusion has arisen regarding mutual funds purchased through a bank.

Once the U.S. banking system got back on its feet after the Great Depression of the 1930s, people began to trust their banks implicitly. Much of this trust came from the fact that checking,

---

1. *Source:* Remarks made to the Consumer Federation of America, Washington, D.C., December 3, 1998.

savings, and other bank investments had the backing of the Federal Deposit Insurance Corporation (FDIC). The FDIC insured deposits and accounts up to $100,000 per customer. For many years, if individuals had more money than that, they either deposited their money in more than one bank or bought government securities.

As the federal mood toward more deregulation developed, banks were allowed to do business in areas that had been the domain of stock brokerage firms. Money market accounts came along, and then banks began to sell mutual funds.

THE TRUST REMAINS

People's trust of banks has remained; however, the trust has led to a misunderstanding. Many investors who buy mutual funds from their bank believe the mutual funds are insured up to $100,000 by the FDIC, and this is not true.

THE RISK IS IDENTICAL, NO MATTER WHO SELLS THEM

Mutual funds have the same risk whether they are sold by a bank, stockbroker, financial adviser, or other marketing organization. They also generally have fees involved.

SEC IS CONCERNED

The SEC is especially concerned because banks currently sell mutual funds that carry the bank's name. The SEC cautions investors that mutual funds sold in banks, including money market funds, are not bank deposits. Individuals buying a stock or bond mutual fund from a bank will usually be aware that it is not insured; the money market fund, however, is more confusing.

SIMILAR BUT DIFFERENT

A good deal of confusion arises because accounts have similar names. Even though one might be called a "money market fund" and the other a "money market deposit account," they are completely different. According to the SEC:

> A money market fund is a type of mutual fund. It is not guaranteed, and comes with a prospectus.

> A money market deposit account is a bank deposit. It is guaranteed, and comes with a Truth in Savings form.

MUTUAL FUNDS ARE NOT DEPOSITS

The fact that mutual funds are not deposits is important. Presently, the vast majority of money market funds earn interest by investing in short-term securities, normally U.S. government securities, but, that could change. The safety of any mutual fund is determined by the fund's strategy, activities, and investments. Mutual funds and the interest they pay are not the same as bank deposits and are not insured by the FDIC.

CHAPTER 15

Invest in What You Understand

Warren Buffett, the billionaire from Omaha and head of the legendary Berkshire Hathaway, once said he decided not to invest in Microsoft Corp. because he didn't understand the computer business. He went on to say that he wished he had taken the time to learn about the computer business.

Although Mr. Buffett would probably have done well and been happy with the stock of Microsoft, his approach is basically correct. Invest in what you understand. Many investors ignore the stock of the company they work for, believing it not to be the best investment. Instead they often find some exotic company or fund of a highly speculative nature and put in their life savings. They are willing to gamble on something they don't understand instead of investing in something they understand very well.

A BILLION DOLLARS A YEAR

According to the Federal Trade Commission, more than a billion dollars a year is lost to investment swindles. The deals all promise high returns in a short period of time. All too quickly the money and the high returns are gone.

Some recent scams: Ostrich farms—buy a breeding pair and before you know it have a whole flock. Specialty fish farms—have new trout all over the place. High tech—all the developments in telecommunications equipment in recent years have made technology scams more popular. It's easy to sound convincing, because most people have only a basic understanding of the technology.

Some popular scams are touted as "IRA approved." The implication is that if they are approved for individual retirement accounts, they must be safe. The fact is there's no such thing as IRA-approved investments. Virtually anything that can be held in a custodial IRA account is acceptable, although most investment firms have some restrictions on investments they consider inappropriate. Many will not allow any options or other derivatives to be traded in IRA accounts because of both risk to the investor and risk to the firm.

PONZI SCAMS ARE STILL AROUND[1]

A review conducted in March/April by the North American Securities Administrators Association (NASAA) and the Council of Better Business Bureaus (CBBB) uncovered a disturbing pattern of 30 major known or suspected Ponzi schemes involving well over $750 million invested by thousands of Americans in the last three years alone. These mass-scale Ponzi schemes were based in 14 states and appear to have defrauded investors in every state in the nation.[2]

NONSCAM INVESTMENTS

If investors know nothing about commodities investing, they need to either spend the time to learn about the finer points or avoid it all together. If investors know nothing about the Internet, why select funds of Internet stocks?

Peter Lynch, the legendary former manager of Fidelity Magellan Fund and author of investment books, gives a bit of valuable advice on learning about investments. Essentially Mr. Lynch says that people should spend at least as much time researching investments as they do when buying a new refrigerator.

---

1. See also Chapter 3.
2. "The Renaissance of Ponzi Schemes," Better Business Bureau, 1995.

DON'T KNOW ENOUGH

Although many individuals invest in mutual funds because they feel they don't know enough about the stock market, to pick the stock themselves, they still need to learn some basics about the market. At the very least, people putting their hard-earned money into mutual funds should understand the stated objectives of the funds.[3] Is the fund an aggressive growth fund, a growth and income fund, or just an income fund? What does the literature say?

BEFORE INVESTING

Before investing, get a prospectus and statement of additional information. Read them thoroughly and make notes. Develop an understanding of what the mutual fund is trying to accomplish and how. Get more information if necessary.

Actually, it can be helpful to get information on two or three different funds. That permits you to make a comparison, which can be a valuable aid in making a decision to buy.

MUTUAL FUNDS ARE A GOOD CHOICE

Mutual funds are a good investment for those who do not have the time to study and learn all the ins and outs of investing. They are an easy investment to buy and sell, but individuals need to have some understanding of the differences between one fund and another. For example, if an investor is in a high tax bracket, a fund paying out taxable income might not be the best selection. If an individual lives on pension and social security payments, aggressive growth is probably not a suitable selection. Even with mutual funds, some study and learning is still essential to good and suitable investing.

---

3. See also Chapter 17.

CHAPTER 16

If You Can't Get Complete Information, Don't Invest

Although they are required to do so, many stockbrokers are resistant to sending out information before making a sale. For brokers who do cold calling, sending out information takes time, which they cannot afford. Brokers are salespeople. Their job is to sell investments, not send out information. When brokers have someone on the phone who asks for information, they consider it a lost sale. Even when they send out information and follow up with a phone call, it's like starting over again. They have to resell the product, and in most cases the investor hasn't read the information.

Nevertheless, brokers will send out information if it's requested. It should always be requested unless the investor knows, trusts, and has worked with the broker on other investments.

MOST ARE HONEST

Most brokers who do cold calling are honest, hard-working, often frustrated individuals. They will be straight with an investor and answer any questions they can. They want the business, but will do their best to match the investment recommendations to the individual's objectives. And, to repeat, they will send out information if asked.

HOW TO HANDLE COLD CALLERS

If you are the recipient of an unwanted cold call and you are not interested, the best thing to do is to say so. Say something like, "I'm not interested, but thanks for calling." Don't request to have information sent unless you have some interest in the product being pitched. A request for information gives the cold caller permission to call again. If you're not interested, it's a waste of time for everyone.

WHEN INTERESTED, GET INFORMATION

An interested investor should get three pieces of information from the cold caller:

1. The broker's name (and phone number)
2. The firm's name
3. A brief description of the investment

Make a note of this preliminary information and call the person back if you're still interested once you have reviewed the literature. Obviously, investors with established brokerage accounts might prefer to invest with their own firm. Cold callers know they are up against such risk, but they will appreciate being informed of the situation.

SOME ARE NOT HONEST

Dishonest cold callers are notorious for refusing to send information. Oftentimes, if any information is sent, it's sketchy, incomplete, and confusing.

IF IT'S A MUTUAL FUND

There has to be a prospectus if a mutual fund is being marketed. Even when there is a prospectus, the investor still needs to be careful. Although the Securities and Exchange Commission takes measures to stop fraudulent activities, it neither approves nor disapproves of any actual securities. However, the SEC does take measures to benefit the investor whenever possible. In 1998, the SEC passed a rule that mutual fund prospectuses had to be in "plain English." Jargon, pointless repetition, and the overuse of legalese are no longer acceptable as of October 1, 1998. The SEC went on to say what was meant by plain English. The following is from new paragraph (d) to Rule 421 (Regulation C) from the Securities and Exchange Commission:

> We require registrants to use plain English principles in the organization, language, and design of the cover page, summary, and risk factors section of their prospectuses.
>
> Registrants must draft the language in these sections so that, at a minimum, it substantially complies with each of the following plain English writing principles:
>
> - active voice;
> - short sentences;
> - definite, concrete, everyday words;
> - tabular presentation or "bullet" lists for complex material, whenever possible;
> - no legal jargon or highly technical business terms; and
> - no multiple negatives.
>
> Registrants can also include other design elements in the prospectus as long as the meaning is reasonably clear.

SEC CLARIFIES THE MEANING

In an effort to move in the same direction as the rule change, the SEC further defined some aspects of plain English. In fact, it made a handbook on the subject, entitled *A Plain English Handbook: How to Create Clear SEC Disclosure Documents*. Anyone can view the handbook on the SEC Internet web site. The Internet address for the handbook is http://www.sec.gov/consumer/plaine.htm.

Although "plain English" can mean different things to different people, the SEC ruling will undoubtedly help investors understand the information in a prospectus.

THE SAI

Investors can also request a statement of additional information (SAI). The SAI contains information not found in the prospectus. It can give a description of the fund advisers and portfolio managers. It also can have specifics on what a mutual fund is trying to accomplish and how it intends to meet its objectives. Information on past performance can also be included.

You can request to have the SAI sent out at the same time a prospectus is sent out. The two documents offer the investor a considerable amount of information concerning a mutual fund.

CHECK ON IT

If something doesn't look right in the information that was sent, the investor can always check the information by calling the Securities and Exchange Commission, the National Association of Securities Dealers, the Better Business Bureau, or the local state attorney general. The time to get information is before the investment is made.

Many people don't begin to check the validity of their investments until something unusual happens to make them suspicious. Oftentimes, by then it's too late and the money is gone. If you can't get complete information up front, don't invest.

Are Big Mutual Funds Better?

Big, bigger, and biggest—for many years banks and brokerage firms have boasted about assets under management as making them better and stronger. Just look at the giants of the mutual fund industry: Fidelity Magellan with its $63 billion, and $10.4 billion in its Fidelity Low-Priced Stock Fund, or Kaufmann with its $6 billion Kaufmann Fund. Money flowed into these funds partly because they were big. "If it's a big fund it must be good" became the assumption of many investors. Remember Ponzi (Chapter 3)? Certainly one of the reasons he did so well was the long line of investors waiting to give him their money. "If he's this popular, he must be good," was probably their assumption.

TOO MUCH POPULARITY

Don't misunderstand. These or any of the large mutual funds should not be directly compared with Ponzi and his shenanigans. He was a crook. Big mutual funds just become carried away with their own popularity. They grow and keep on growing until they become difficult to effectively manage, no matter how many people they hire. For several years the larger mutual funds have been criticized for becoming too large, but still those funds have been slow to close to new investors.

According to Morningstar, a company that analyzes mutual funds, 211 of all existing funds (more than 6,000) have closed to new investors since 1961; however, more than 80 percent of those have closed in the last 4 years. Although the trend is growing, many believe the size limitations on mutual funds are long over-due. When mutual funds get too large, it becomes more difficult to achieve strong performance. The number of companies in the stock market has limitations, and the number of high-performance com-panies is usually small. When the shares of better companies become pricey, portfolio managers are left with two choices. They can buy the highly priced stock or lower their standards. Either one can have a negative impact on performance.

THE 5 PERCENT RULE

There are SEC restrictions placed on any person or entity own-ing more than 5 percent of any one company's stock. That means mutual funds limit themselves to 5 percent stock ownership of any company. This limitation, added to the need for high per-formance, significantly increases the difficulty level for giant mutual funds.

LOWER STANDARDS

Eventually, the portfolio manager has to lower the stan-dards, just to find something to buy. When the standards are low-ered, performance will eventually suffer. Because the large fund buys lower-quality stocks, the price action attracts the attention of other buyers. Prices rise and the stocks become overvalued. As long as there are buyers, the prices will continue to rise; but when the buyers taper off and the value is examined, the situation can attract sellers.

LIQUIDITY PROBLEMS

Liquidity problems are especially pronounced in the smaller-cap funds. If a mega mutual fund takes a large position in a small com-pany, with a modest daily trading volume, selling could become a real problem. Liquidating an entire position would likely not receive a decent price, and selling over time could push the price constantly lower. Managers can only combat liquidity problems by investing in larger companies or by increasing the number of companies in the portfolio.

In 1995, the Kaufmann Fund had $1.6 billion in assets; in 1998, the fund had more than $6 billion. The number of companies in the portfolio went from 272 to 451.[1] The managers doubled their workload. Although the fund avoided potential liquidity problems by increasing the number of investments, it's hard to believe that quality wasn't compromised in the process.

REDEMPTIONS

Redemptions are the dread of all mutual fund portfolio managers. When mutual fund investors sell, they redeem their shares and are paid the net asset value. Mutual funds keep some assets in cash or cash equivalents, just to pay the regular ongoing redemptions. However, if the stock market experiences a sharp correction or slides into a decline, the redemptions generally increase dramatically. In order to pay investors, the fund's portfolio manager has to liquidate some stock positions. Selling stock forces the prices of the stock even lower, which can attract even more redemptions.

Much of the crash of 1987 is attributed to mutual fund redemptions. Mutual fund holders panicked and sold their holdings, thus hammering the weak market down even farther. Although in recent corrections, most fund holders have either held position or bought more, there still have been a significant number of sellers. Obviously, a large number of sellers can be detrimental to a fund manager's strategy. If the manager has to sell 200,000 shares of a company, the price will be more damaged than if it were only necessary to sell 10,000 shares. As the mutual fund receives lower and lower prices for the stock it is selling, the fund's NAV drops continually lower. A lowered NAV means investors have larger losses.

---

1. Maria Atanasov, "Why Funds Should Swear Off Asset Growth," *Fortune Investor*, March 3, 1998.

LARGER DOESN'T MEAN BETTER

Superlarge mutual funds develop difficulties in regard to selection and liquidity. This is especially true of the smaller-capitalization mutual funds. They run out of good-performance companies to buy, and in downturns can have a hard time selling.

Publicity and the popularity of large funds contribute much to their high performance. As more investor money comes into the fund, the managers buy more stock for the portfolio. The buying causes the stock prices to rise, and that in turn causes the price of the fund to rise, without any corresponding increase in values. Some of this growth can be absorbed, but market efficiencies can catch up and turn the situation around. The resulting decline will probably be more devastating to the large funds than to funds that are more modest in size.

CHAPTER 18

Invest According to Objectives

"I want to make a lot of money in the stock market, but I don't want to take risk." Is this statement an objective or a wish? Since an objective is something you should be able to measure, the statement is assuredly a wish. However, a wish can be redefined as an objective.

WHAT MAKES A GOOD OBJECTIVE?

Oftentimes, such things as retirement, children's college education, a house, or a new car are stated as objectives for investing. Even they are too general, although they are more specific than "a lot of money." What about a set time for achievement? Retirement and children's education have built-in time periods; however, it's a good idea to break many of these large (10- or 20-year) blocks of time into smaller segments like 5 years or possibly 10 years. Shorter time periods help to ensure that performance is being evaluated and that investments are being adjusted to the most current market realities.

WHAT DECISIONS NEED TO BE MADE?

In order to meet an investment objective, certain information is essential. What specifically will be done? What performance is acceptable in the current market? What stock funds will be purchased? How much diversification is necessary to moderate risk (how many funds)? What time frame should be used? How will success be measured? When these questions are answered, it's time to formulate an objective.

An objective should:

Be specific.   What activities will be done to choose investments?

Be reasonable in expectations.   Base expectations on observable performance.

Consider risk.   Select funds and diversify to a comfort level.

Have a time frame.   One year, two years, five years, and so on.

Be measurable.   Performance needs to be measured to be evaluated.

CATEGORIES OF STOCK

When stockbrokers open new accounts, they are required by Rule 4054 of the NYSE to know their customer. That means they need to know certain details about the person's investing experience, financial status, and, most importantly, investment objectives. In order to standardize objectives into mutually understood concepts, they usually list four categories:

Income.   Refers to income from dividends or interest payments

Growth.   Looks for price growth, usually newer companies that pay no dividends

Total return.   Looks for price growth and income from dividends

Speculation.   Looks for short-term trades with quick profits (e.g., new companies, small companies in rapid growth areas, turnarounds, and other speculative situations)

ALL INVESTMENTS FIT

Income, growth, total return, and speculation—all financial investments fit into these categories. Mutual funds have an advantage over stocks for investors establishing an objective. Funds are constructed according to an investment objective, which means it's easy for the investor to match a fund to his or her own objective. Common stocks don't usually state an investment objective. It's up to the investor to figure out which stocks fit into his or her objective and strategy.

MUTUAL FUND ADVANTAGE

Mutual funds not only state an objective; they state an investment strategy as well.

Oftentimes a mutual fund objective is stated in general terms. Therefore, it's usually necessary to do some digging into the statement of strategy as well as description of risk. However, the stated investment objective can help an investor write out his or her own objective.

FUND OBJECTIVES

Here are some examples of mutual fund objectives.

Income

Fund name: Fidelity Intermediate Bond Fund

Fund objective: "High current income. As with any mutual fund, there is no assurance that the fund will achieve its goal."[1]

We immediately learn two things by looking at the name of the fund and its stated objective.

1. The words "Intermediate Bond Fund" say that interest rate risk is moderated by the fund's selection of maturity dates. Intermediate-term bonds don't have as much reinvestment risk as short-term bonds, and there is less risk that rising interest rates will cause share prices to decline.

---

1. Fidelity Investments Online,
    http://personal361.fidelity.com/gen/mflfid/9/315912105.html.

2. The words "High current income" are clues that the fund is taking some risk for higher yields.

Fund Strategy: "Normally invests in investment-grade debt securities while maintaining an average maturity of three to 10 years. FMR uses the Lehman Brothers Intermediate Government/Corporate Bond Index as a guide in structuring the fund and selecting its investments."

The word "Normally" suggests that it might be worthwhile to check the current portfolio. The suggestion is that the fund can invest in below-investment-grade securities.

Fund Risk: "The fund's yield, share price, and total return change daily and are based on interest rates, market conditions, other economic and political news, and on the quality and maturity of its investments. In general, bond prices rise when interest rates fall, and vice versa. This effect is usually more pronounced for longer-term securities. You may have a gain or loss when you sell your shares."

Although this is an income fund, it is not the most conservative, nor is it the most speculative. It is somewhere in between the two ends of the spectrum. The expected yield when the investor purchases the fund should be higher than intermediate-term U.S. Treasury bonds. It's difficult to determine how much higher, but the investor must believe the higher yield is worth the extra risk involved.

At the end of February 1999, the 30-year U.S. Treasury bond had a yield of 5.57 percent, the 30-day yield on this fund was 5.50 percent, the 5-year bond was yielding 5.21 percent, and the 10-year bond was at 5.29 percent. There was a difference, but it was not much of a difference. The 3-month T-bill was down at a 4.55 percent yield. In order to significantly increase income as compared with U.S. Treasury bonds, the investor had to consider more risk, with either a high-yield bond fund or a possibly a combination growth and income fund. In fairness, this was a time when interest rates were low and it was difficult to find much difference with fixed-income investments. The yield may in fact have been enough when the greater safety of the intermediate-term securities was added to considerations.

Investor Income Objective: Here is an example of how an investment objective could be stated.

Invest $10,000 in an intermediate-term bond fund to gain an expected yield of $\frac{1}{2}$ to 1 percent higher than the 3-month Treasury bill yield over the next 3 to 5 years.

This objective could be part of a larger income objective, with the rest of the assets invested in other areas, possibly short- to intermediate-term Treasury bonds. With this objective, the investor knows why the mutual fund was purchased and precisely how to evaluate the annual performance.

Growth

Investor's Growth Objective:

Invest $10,000 in a fund for capital appreciation for the next 5 to 10 years. Performance should match or better the 5-year average but not be less than the 10-year average. As compared with the market, the fund should match or better the annual percent increase of the S&P 500 Index.

Total Return

Investor Total Return Objective:

Invest $10,000 for total return in a growth and income fund, for the next 5 to 10 years. Performance will be expected to match the past 5 years annual total return, in relation to the overall stock market performance. At a minimum, the fund should be expected to better the 10-year average annual total return. Risk is moderated by the dividend-paying stocks in the fund's portfolio.

At the end of each year, or more often, the investor can look at his or her stated objective and remember what was expected when the fund was purchased. A comparison of the fund performance with this objective gives the investor a quick and easy evaluation.

Speculation

Investor's Speculation Objective:

Invest $10,000 for the next 3 to 5 years in an aggressive growth fund. Expect an annual return comparable to the fund's 5-year average or at least to match the Russell Midcap Growth Index (5-year average).

Here we set the minimum standard to the benchmark because the lifetime average is higher than the 5-year average.

EASY EVALUATION

When the objectives are set specifically, evaluation becomes an easy exercise. Either the performance is higher, the same as, or lower than the benchmarks established. If the fund performance is lower, the investor can dig deeper to find the reason and arrive at a decision whether or not to keep the fund.

EVALUATION OF OBJECTIVES

Personal investment objectives for mutual funds should be examined at least annually. Compare the fund performance with the expected performance stated in the objective. If performance is below expectations, find out why. Is it the market or the sector, or is something wrong with the fund's management? A decision must then be reached. Should the fund be sold, or is it time to buy more shares? If additional shares are purchased, adding a few comments to the objective notes will be helpful for follow-up evaluations.

CHAPTER 19

Past Performance Is No Guarantee

Mutual funds use a disclaimer in their literature. Essentially, the disclaimer says that past performance is not a guarantee of future results. Additionally the disclaimer might say something to the effect that the investor's principal might be worth more or less when the shares are redeemed (sold).

Disclaimer statements used to be printed in bold capital letters. They made the statement stand out from the rest of the information, but that also made it more difficult to read and understand. As part of the new "plain English" recommendations from the Securities and Exchange Commission, the statements don't usually appear in caps anymore.

WHAT DOES THE DISCLAIMER MEAN TO THE INVESTOR?

It means the investor might lose money or make money. Any record of performance may indicate a well-managed fund, but it cannot guarantee what will happen in the future. The only thing certain in life is change. Good past performance might have been the result of factors other than good portfolio management. A strong stock market, such as existed in the mid-to-late 1990s, made all fund managers look like geniuses. Really, all they had to do was buy in accordance with their fund objectives and hang on. There wasn't much "management" necessary.

APPROVAL-DISAPPROVAL STATEMENT

Another disclaimer appearing in the mutual fund prospectus is the approval-disapproval statement. It might appear in all capital letters or it might not.

> Neither the Securities and Exchange Commission nor any state securities commission has approved or disapproved of these securities or passed upon the accuracy or adequacy of this prospectus. Any representation to the contrary is a criminal offense.[1]

Unscrupulous or overanxious brokers and other representatives selling mutual funds have been known to attest to the safety of securities by indicating that they were approved by the SEC or state regulatory agencies. Although the SEC is involved with the issuance of securities, it neither approves nor disapproves of the actual securities. Anyone who says otherwise is breaking the law. The SEC wants investors to be aware of this fact, which is why the statement appears in the mutual fund prospectus.

FUNDS WANT INVESTORS TO BE AWARE

Mutual funds normally want investors to be aware of the investment risks. Still, representatives tend to downplay or understate risks for a simple reason. If they spend too much time explaining risk, they'll never sell anything. Many investors overreact to risk discussions and don't invest with the conscientious representative who explains the risk. These investors often turn around and invest in unsuitable, high-risk investments where risk was never discussed.

Some funds are adding additional information regarding risk. The Vanguard US Growth Fund places a small flag symbol throughout its prospectus. Wherever the flag appears, a detailed description of risk also appears. It enables the investor to understand the risks involved with investing in the fund. For example, a flag on page 5 of the prospectus says:

> Because the Fund invests a higher percentage of assets in its ten largest holdings than the average stock fund does, the Fund is sub-

---

1. Prospectus for Vanguard US Growth Fund, December 29, 1998.

ject to the risk that its performance may be hurt disproportionately by the poor performance of relatively few stocks.[2]

Statements like this do much to detail the risk of fund investing. The statement points out a risk that many investors would not realize otherwise. An investor who understands this risk factor is also likely to understand why the stock market might be up when the fund is down. That understanding can be a benefit to the fund.

BE AWARE

It's always better to be aware of risk. Investors can lose a large amount of money because they didn't want to hear about risk. But keep risk in perspective. Investors who are too risk aversive often end up with a low, safe return.

Although past performance never guarantees future results, it's the only performance information available. That means past performance should not be discounted either.

---

2. Ibid.

CHAPTER 20

Check Frequently to Avoid Fraud

The most outrageous lies that can be invented will find believers if a man only tells them with all his might.

Mark Twain

Sometimes even telling lies with all one's might isn't necessary. We all have a weakness toward believing things we want to hear. People want to hear that their children are brilliant and beautiful. They want to hear how prudent, how intelligent, and how perceptive they are when presented an investment opportunity. Many people also have a basic trust of others, especially when it comes to investing.

There are people out there who make large amounts of money based on the trust of others. Although many are legitimate and strive to make money for their clients by providing investments to achieve objectives, there are also a few who desire to only make money for themselves. Fraud has existed for a long time; it's probably older than money. Although regulators work to stop scams, investors should be wary of unusual opportunities or situations.

EVEN FRIENDS

Some perpetrators of fraud even prey on people who have become their friends. They have accepted large amounts of money to be invested, sometimes in legitimate mutual funds, and have pocketed the money instead. A few have even gone so far as to make dummy statements using stationery copied from the mutual fund. The investors received the monthly statements and believed everything was good.

It was only when the statements stopped coming that the investors became suspicious. Imagine the sinking feeling of calling a well-known mutual fund company to inquire about missing a statement for the past 3 months, only to learn that there is no record of the $30,000 investment. The trusted "friend" never sent the money to buy shares in the fund. All the statements were phony.

HOW TO CHECK

The North American Securities Administrators Association in Washington, D.C., advises the following checks for investors as a way to protect against fraud.[1]

1. Investigate the investment adviser and salesperson thoroughly.
   A. Call a state securities agency to find out if an adviser is properly licensed to provide investment advice.
   B. If the adviser also is licensed as a stockbroker, background information should be available through a state securities agency from the Central Registration Depository (CRD). The CRD is a computerized reference system operated jointly by the North American Securities Administrators Association and the National Association of Securities Dealers.
   C. The phone number of the state securities administrator appears in most telephone books under state government.
2. Is the investment opportunity registered for sale in the state in which you live?
   A. Call the state securities agency to find out. All investment opportunities must be registered or exempt. If a recommended investment isn't registered or exempt, consider it a big warning flag and check further or forget it.

---

1. "How to Protect Your Money from Theft by Dishonest Investment Advisers," North American Securities Administrators Association, September 1997, http://www.nasaa.org/investoredu/investoralerts/iafraud.html

B. Ask for written "disclosure" information. Review the information very carefully and understand the risks involved. Keep asking until you understand. If pressured by an investment adviser to make a quick decision, say no. There are other investments.

3. Always stay in charge of the money.

A. Protect that nest egg. If the world of investments is difficult to understand, take time to become educated.

B. Read one or more of the many magazines devoted to personal finance on a regular basis. Get books on investing.

C. Once the investment is made, carefully review the account statement. Make sure to know where the money is being held. Generally, account statements come from the custodian of the securities as well as an investment adviser. Check to see that all transactions appearing on the statement were personally authorized.

4. Con artists are often extremely polite.

A. Successful swindlers can present professional-sounding sales pitches that seem safe. It's as safe as putting money in the bank, so they say.

B. These swindlers can be extremely polite, might dress in expensive clothes, and might work out of impressive offices with prestigious addresses.

C. Many seek prospects at houses of worship, country clubs, or senior centers—places where people tend to trust each other.

D. Others might first provide a sound financial service and then move in for the kill. Before turning over any money, call the state securities administrator and check out the salesperson.

5. Keep greed in check.

A. If an investment sounds too good to be true, it probably is. No matter how often this caveat is repeated, the idea doesn't seem to sink into investors' memory.

B. A legitimate adviser should learn about the investor's financial needs and goals, as well as a comfortable level of risk. Then a "suitable investment" should be suggested, not sold.

C. Don't allow the promise of high returns to cloud your judgment. Many people believe there is a secret to successful investing that will make them rich overnight. The only secret to investing is that it should be done prudently.

D. Con artists play upon the imagination and dreams of people.

6. Keep notes of every phone conversation and meeting.

A. It's important to keep a record of conversations and meetings with an investment adviser.

B. Con artists prefer an atmosphere of trust rather than carefully maintained records.

C. Write down the date, time, and place, as well. Don't rely on memory.

MORE ON CHECKING

1. Be suspicious of anything unusual. In one fraud case an investor became suspicious when the monthly statement was hand delivered rather than mailed.

2. Call the Better Business Bureau and ask if any complaints have been filed.

3. Stay with mainline investing and avoid the fringes.

4. If you have invested in a well-known mutual fund company, call the company to check on the account.

5. Expect a return related to the market performance.

6. Ask about risk until you fully understand it.

BE AWARE

Be aware that fraud exists. Avoid it by taking the time to check out the person or organization doing the promotion.

CHAPTER 21

Small Stocks Make the "January Effect"

Investors have traded the "January effect" for many years. The effect is a noticeable tendency for smaller-company share prices to rally in the first month of the year.

> THE JANUARY EFFECT, for those few investors who haven't already heard about it, is the pronounced tendency for all stocks, but especially those of small-cap companies, to perform well during the first few weeks of the new year.[1]

WHY DOES IT HAPPEN?

Although the answer to this question is somewhat debated, the consensus opinion seems to be that tax-loss selling at the end of the year leaves individual investors with cash. In January, they rebuild their portfolios, often with the smaller companies. There also appears to be some positive influence after a Democrat is elected president, possibly because Democrats tend to have an antitrust leaning.

---

1. Mark Hulbert, "The Case for Small Caps," Wall Street Irregular, *Forbes*, December 1996, http://www.forbes.com/forbes/121696/5814392a.htm.

WHO'S SELLING AND BUYING?

Logic says it's the individual investors, those who can take advantage of tax-loss selling. Institutions generally don't need the strategy.

> Only individual investors—the bulk of small stock owners—worry about taxes since institutional investors are exempt. That fact has made small stocks perform better than larger ones since at least World War II.[2]

The January effect is indirectly influenced by large institutional investors. The large portfolio managers are paid in relation to their performance. Near year-end, they have a tendency to avoid the riskier small-capitalization companies in favor of the large conservative ones.

Oftentimes, small issues return 6.8 percent in January, with the larger-company shares returning less than 2 percent. Small stocks are those that have a market capitalization of $150 million to $200 million. Market capitalization is calculated by multiplying the market price times the number of shares outstanding.

INSTITUTIONAL PAY INFLUENCE

The way Wall Street's largest institutional investors are paid also influences the January effect. The large portfolio managers earn their bonus and salaries based on how well they perform. Performance frequently is measured using the larger-cap companies in the Standard & Poor's 500 Index as a benchmark. (See Figure 21-1.) Whereas during the year they are willing to take more risk (especially in January), coming up on the end of the year is the time to be conservative.

> According to Professors Robert Haugen and Philippe Jorion of the University of California, Irvine, these compensation packages encourage managers in the last months of the year to lock in their relative gains by mimicking the S&P 500. Consequently, their incen-

2. Paola Banchero, "So-Called January Effect Is Looking Good for Investors," *Kansas City Business Journal*, December 30, 1996, http://www.amcity.com/kansascity/stories/123096/story4.html.

FIGURE 21-1

The January Effect, the Difference between the S&P 500
Index and the S&P Low Priced Stocks. (*Data source:* Yale
Hirsch, *The 1999 Stock Trader's Almanac,* The Hirsch Organization.)

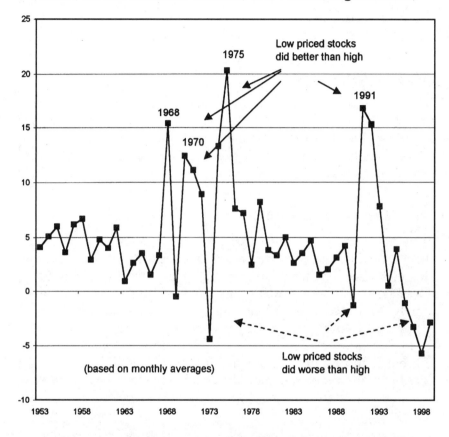

tives to purchase small-cap stocks outside the S&P 500 will be lowest in December and highest in January.[3]

Professors Haugen and Jorion further believe the growing
dominance of institutional portfolio managers will perpetuate the
existence of the January effect. However, although opinions of
experts are fine, the evidence suggests the January effect could be
changing. Anytime a consistent trading pattern receives publicity,
there are many investors who will try to take advantage of the situation—thus changing the pattern.

---

3. Hulbert, "The Case for Small Caps."

Keep in mind that the chart in Figure 21-1 shows only the percentage difference between the two indexes. The difference showed phenomenal success in 1968, at 15.4 percent. It also did well in the early and mid-1970s and in 1991–1992. Although a quick look might suggest a decline in the January effect from the mid-1970s to 1990, a similar occurrence took place in the years between 1955 and 1966.

HAS IT GONE AWAY?

Of great concern is the 1996–1998 period when the small companies were in negative territory. The last significant move was back in 1992. Could it be that the time-honored January effect has traded itself away or has moved? If it has taken a temporary hiatus, where did it go and will it return?

WHERE DID IT GO?

Some say the January effect should be renamed the "December effect" because it now occurs in the last month of the year. However, they may be confusing the January effect with the "Santa Claus rally." Others say it's just delayed to February or even March. What does the evidence show?

As you can see from the increases in the Standard & Poor's Small Cap Index shown in Figure 21-2, it appears that the January effect has moved in part to the following month of February. Possibly it should be renamed the "February effect."

The two main reasons given for the existence of the January effect are :

- Tax-loss selling in December by individuals, who reposition their assets in January
- Portfolio managers aligning their positions closer to the Standard & Poor's 500 Index toward the end of the year to dress up the results.

If the two causes given are correct, it would make more sense for the January effect to move to February or March rather than occur in December. Look at the effect on the daily prices of a mutual fund (Figure 21-3).

FIGURE 21-2

Standard & Poor's Small Cap Index,
December 1994–February 1999.

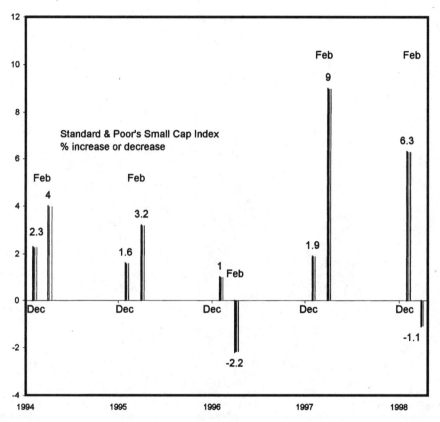

INCONCLUSIVE EVIDENCE

That the January effect has existed in the past is irrefutable. That it still exists in 1999 is questionable. The evidence shown here suggests that the traditional buying of small-capitalization companies in the month of January has changed. Some of it has moved to February and later in the year. Some analysts believe the effect has suffered because of the recent popularity of larger companies.

FIGURE 21-3

The February Effect, Putnam OTC Emerging Growth Fund,
1995–1999.

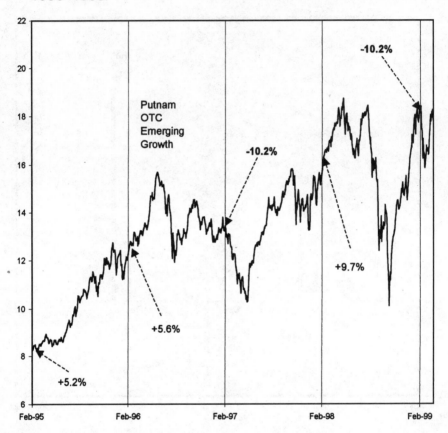

WILL IT REAPPEAR?

Time will show whether or not the small-company January effect
will reappear. It's part of the speculation that goes with smaller
companies and trying to profit from short-term strategies. The
individual investor should approach this strategy like all others,
with knowledge and the realization that it might fail to occur.
However, in the 46 years covered by the chart in Figure 21-1, only
7 years were below the gain on the large-cap Standard & Poor's
500. Still, 4 of the 7 were in the most recent years. The only thing
certain in the stock market is change.

CHAPTER 22

There's Always a Year-End Sell-Off

The word "always" in the chapter title is a tip off. Things are seldom described as *always* in the stock market. The fact is, most years experience some kind of selling near the end of the year, but *most* is not the same as *always*. Sometimes the selling is significant, other times it's minor, and once in awhile sell-off is nonexistent at the end of a year.

A sell-off at the end of the year is also referred to as "tax-loss selling," based on the belief that some investors are selling stocks that are trading at losing prices. Additionally, investors might be selling stocks with disappointing price performance. Whatever the reason, the event does occur with some regularity.

AFTER THE 25TH

To place some consistency on a definition of year-end, we will look primarily at selling during the final week of the year, basically December 26 to 31. Some only consider the final trading day of the year as a true year-end sell-off. It appears as though many investors are selling prior to the end of the year. Evidence of this can also be seen on the charts.

WHAT GOOD IS THE KNOWLEDGE?

If an investor has a poor-performing mutual fund, it is probably best to unload it before the year-end selling begins, possibly in a

Santa Claus rally (Chapter 40). If an investor is looking for bargains in stock or mutual fund prices, those bargains might be available near the end of the year. One of the basic concepts of investing in stock is to buy when others are selling. However, the buying strategy has a tax consideration. Many funds make capital distributions near the end of the year. Some investors might wish to avoid this taxable event. Distribution information is available from the mutual funds.

THE DOW INDUSTRIAL AVERAGE AND THE STANDARD & POOR'S 500 INDEX

Both the Dow Industrial Average and the Standard & Poor's 500 Index appear on the chart shown in Figure 22-1. The left scale is for the Dow and the right scale is for the S&P 500. One trading day of November is included, with the daily closing levels of December for the years 1994 through 1998.

1994

Indecisive, that's the word for 1994. The stock market ran into a brick wall between 3,900 and 4,000 on the Dow Industrial Average. The wall for the S&P 500 was between 470 and 480 points. Although some significant selling continued into the early part of December, a rigorous Santa rally put the Dow Industrials into positive territory for the year, up 80.35 points. The sell-off at the end resulted in a drop of only 28.26 points for the Dow Industrial Average. The Standard & Poor's 500 Index ended the year down 7 points. Year-end selling amounted to only 3.2 points for the S&P 500.

1994 Total Year Results

Dow Industrial Average up	80.35
Standard & Poor's 500 Index	−7.00

A Significant Rally

The rally at the end of 1994 became important for the next few years. The rally continued, more than doubling the Dow Industrial Average and coming within 50 points of tripling the S&P 500 Index by 1998. Even so, there was a small sell-off at the end of 1994.

FIGURE 22-1

Year-End Sell-Off, Dow Industrial Average and S&P 500
Index, 1994–1999.

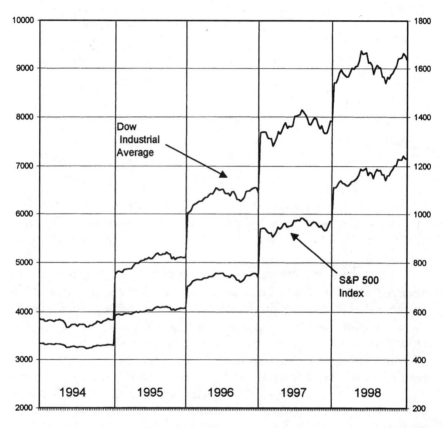

1995

The rally that started in late 1994 continued through 1995, to make
it a year of new highs in the stock market indexes and averages.
Interest rates, which rose considerably in 1994, were being pressured lower. Gains existed in the broad market as well: The NAS-
DAQ Composite Index, which showed a nearly 25-point decline in
1994, was up just over 300 points for 1995. The Russell 2000 Index,
which had been down 15.44 the previous year, now closed up 69.49
points. The Dow Industrials closed the year just over 33 percent,

and a more than 34 percent gain appeared in the Standard & Poor's 500 Index.

With such gains in major indexes, it would only make sense that some selling would occur at the end of the year (Figure 22-1). A rather strong sell-off appeared in the Dow Industrial Average in mid-December, with just a small year-end correction. The pattern suggests that many investors were trying to avoid selling at the very end of the year.

1995 Total Year Results
Dow Industrial Average up   1,282.68
S&P 500 Index up   156.66

1996

In terms of strong market growth, 1996 was a repeat of the previous year. All major indexes showed significant increases. The Dow was up 26 percent, and the S&P 500 followed close behind, up 20 percent.

The year-end selling was also similar to that of the previous year (1995). There was a big sell-off early in December and a smaller decline at the end of the month. This pattern is obvious in both the Dow and the S&P 500. There was a 100-point sell-off on the Dow Industrials at year-end, a much smaller decline compared with the stronger correction of 253.35 points earlier in December. And there was a 15.08-point sell-off on the S&P 500 Index at year-end; this is also a much smaller decline compared with a 36-point sell-off in early December. Obviously, the better time to buy stock mutual funds was in the early December correction.

1996 Total Year Results
Dow Industrial Average up   1,331.15
S&P 500 Index up   124.81

1997

Although 1997 closed the year with the Dow Industrials up 20 percent and the S&P 500 Index up 34 percent, the year-end sell-off started in early December and continued into the last week of the year. The Dow dropped 489 points in the sell-off, then rallied about half of that (255.84 points), and had a small sell-off at the end. The S&P 500 Index dropped just over 51 points and recovered more than 38, with a similar selling session at the end.

December would have been an excellent month for buying a stock mutual fund, especially in that last week of the year.

1997 Total Year Results*
Dow Industrial Average up   1,459.98
S&P 500 Index up   229.69

*Both indicators had a minor sell-off at year-end.

1998

With a now familiar pattern, December 1998 showed a sell-off early in the month (Figure 22-1), with a smaller correction right at year-end. The Dow was up a healthy 16 percent, and the Standard & Poor's 500 Index rose 27 percent.

The Dow corrected 437.94 points in early December and then turned back around and rallied another 625.38 points. The last two days of the month experienced a sell-off of 139.55 points. The S&P Index fell only 47 points in early December and then rallied more than 100 points. The rally peaked at 1,241.81, after which there was another sell-off to close the year at 1,229.23, up 259 points for the year.

WHAT CONCLUSIONS CAN BE DRAWN?

Based on the major indicators of the Dow Industrial Average and the Standard & Poor's 500 Index from 1994 through 1998, selling at the end of a year can be light and insignificant. However, investors can look for a stronger sell-off earlier in December.

Although the early December selling appears to be developing a pattern of occurrence, it should not be relied upon to always happen. Such patterns evolve from time to time and then disappear. They vanish when too many stock traders attempt to trade the pattern.

REASON OTHER THAN TRADING

Year-end selling, whether in the last month or the last week of the year, is reasonably consistent. It is possibly caused both by professional managers who are trimming their portfolios and by individuals who are selling for tax write-off losses before the end of the year.

Individuals buying mutual funds can be alert to the possibility of a December sell-off and time their purchases accordingly. However, before buying, find out if there will be any taxable distributions of capital before the end of the year.

Government Bond Funds Are Not Guaranteed

Sadly, confusion about the government guaranteeing bond funds has long been fostered by desperate representatives trying to make a difficult sale. They have a nervous prospect on the phone. The investor's objective is income with preservation of capital. A government bond fund can nearly match this objective, but with a few important exceptions.

Because the representative knows the prospect is concerned with safety, a statement similar to the following will eventually be made. "This is a government bond fund, containing only securities that are guaranteed by the full faith and credit of the United States government." Is it a lie? No, not exactly. Is the statement accurate? Yes it is, in most situations.

So what's the problem? Why shouldn't a sales representative make such a statement? Because something important has been omitted from the "government guarantee" statement. Although the securities in the fund are guaranteed by the government, the government cannot guarantee the prices of the securities. The share prices of the fund are based on the prices of the securities. These prices can change every day. If interest rates drop, the price of the fund goes up. But if interest rates go up, the price of the fund goes down, and that could mean a loss if the shares have to be sold, if the investor needs to raise the cash.

HOW MUCH DO PRICES FLUCTUATE?

The amount of price fluctuation in a government bond fund can vary from fund to fund. Primarily it will depend on the composition of the portfolio. Certainly, the fluctuation of interest rates will cause prices to fluctuate.

Everyone is usually well aware of changes in the highly publicized "prime rate," which is the interest rate charged by commercial banks for loans to their best customers. Although the prime rate only changes periodically, other interest rates change daily. If we look at the calculated yields of the 30-year U.S. Treasury bond, we see they change on a daily basis (Figure 23-1).

The effects of the pressure to lower interest rates in the 1989–1999 period are easily observed. The percent yield on the long bond dropped more than 3 percent between 1990 and 1993. Then in late October 1993, an upward move in interest rates pushed the 30-year yield from 5.83 percent to 8.14 percent during the year that followed. That much of an increase had an impact on the prices of government securities.

MARKET RISK

Market risk with a government securities fund is the possibility of a price decline caused by rising interest rates. The net asset value of these funds is recalculated every business day. If interest rates have moved up, the share prices are lowered. If interest rates drop, the share prices are raised.

NO MATURITY DATE

Another disadvantage to an open-end bond mutual fund is the fact that the securities cannot be held to maturity. When owning the actual government bonds, even if the market price declines, the bonds can be held until they mature. The bondholder is unaffected by price changes as long as the bonds are not sold.

With a mutual fund of bonds, there is no effective maturity date. If interest rates rise, the mutual fund share prices will decline. However, because interest rates rise and fall frequently over a period of time (Figure 23-1), the investor with a long-term plan should not sell mutual fund shares with every price fluctuation.

FIGURE 23-1

30-Year Treasury Bond Yields.

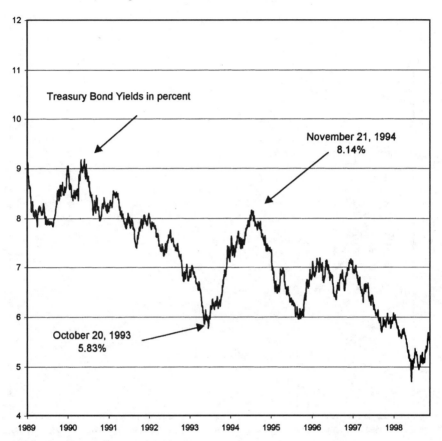

GOVERNMENT BOND FUND PRICES

Observing the price trend of a typical government bond fund shows the price impact of higher interest rates. The Fidelity Government Income Fund price dropped from $7.715 a share to $6.893 in November 1994. That's a 12 percent decline in the net asset value and probably caused concern among several investors. As Figure 23-2 shows, however, it was definitely not the time to sell.

FIGURE 23-2

Fidelity Government Income Fund.

BE AWARE OF THE RISK

The main point is to be aware that risk is involved when buying a mutual fund containing U.S. Treasury bonds. The prices will fluctuate with changes in interest rates. When interest rates increase, the bond fund prices will decline. When interest rates drop, the bond fund prices will increase.

CHAPTER 24

Never Buy a Fund from a Voice

Knowing that the oldest mutual fund dates from 1924 makes one wonder why mutual funds didn't start earlier. Perhaps it was because of the lack of telephones. There were money "pools" before 1924—some of them quite large and powerful. Many were trying to hit the next "corner" on gold; others just wanted huge profits from the stock market. Possibly, mutual funds couldn't get a good start until the telephone was more widespread. With the telephone, sales reps could reach out and touch people for money to invest. The phone enabled them to reach the masses of people in order to find the few who had both the money and the interest to invest in the stock market.

WHAT IS MEANT BY "VOICE"?

Never buy anything from just a voice, investments or otherwise. What that means is simply get information. Check out the company selling the funds or other investments. Pay the "voice" a visit and see what the person is like; see if he or she will take the time to get to know you and your investment objectives.

ASK FOR INFORMATION

It can't be stressed too much. Ask, ask, and ask for information on any investment idea that sounds interesting. However, don't waste the representative's time; if you're not interested, say so. But if you are interested, get the information and check it out before you hand over any money.

HOW TO GET RID OF A BROKER

Here are some easy statements to end a conversation with an unwanted call from a broker:

- I'm sorry, but I'm just not interested. Thank you for calling, though.
- I don't have any money to invest.
- I have a friend who is a broker.
- I have a relative who is a broker.
- I'm perfectly satisfied with my current account executive.

IT'S A NUMBERS GAME

Most brokers play the cold-calling game by the numbers. They know if they make a certain number of calls in a day, they will get a small amount of business. If they get lucky, they may get a large amount of business. It's "dialing for dollars" as far as they are concerned. Many will make no attempt or merely a token attempt to discern an investor's objectives or ability to invest. The only thing that keeps them on the line is encouragement. Anything that suggests interest in their company, product, or investing in general will keep these cold callers hanging in.

At any time, a person can end the conversation by boldly saying, "I'm sorry, but I'm just not interested." Thanking the broker for calling is not really necessary, but it does take some of the bite out of the rejection.

LET THEM KNOW WHAT YOU WANT

If the objective has been defined and it's time to gather information, fine. Tell the caller what you want. A broker will be surprised, if not shocked, when an investor comes back with, "I'm glad you called. My investment objective for the next 16 years is to invest for my son's college education. I'm looking to find a conservative growth and income fund, with reasonable management fees and a low sales charge, no more than 4 percent. What do you have in that area?" If the sales representative is quick enough to field the comment and suggest a fund, request that a prospectus and statement of additional information be sent out.

Above all, do *not* buy during that first phone call. Yes, market timing can be important, but risk can be even more important. Until you review the information, there is no way to know how much risk might be involved. Get the information and examine it well. If you're interested, call the broker back and buy the fund, with the knowledge of exactly what you are buying.

CHAPTER 25

If a Bank Sells a Mutual Fund, It's Not Insured

When people talk about bank insurance, they're usually referring to FDIC insurance. The Federal Deposit Insurance Corporation insures bank depositors up to $100,000. However, not every investment sold by banks is covered. There is a deep concern among regulatory agencies because they are finding that many people who buy mutual funds from a bank believe the investments are covered by FDIC insurance, and they are not.

WHAT'S NOT INSURED?

Treasury Securities

Among items an investor might buy or keep at a bank that are not insured are Treasury securities, including Treasury bills (T-bills), notes, and bonds. T-bills are more commonly purchased through a financial institution.

Although Treasury securities are not covered by federal deposit insurance, payments of interest and principal (including redemption proceeds) on Treasury securities that are deposited to an investor's deposit account at an insured depository institution are covered by FDIC insurance up to the $100,000 limit. And even though there is no federal insurance on Treasury securities, the securities are backed by the full faith and credit of the U.S.

government—the strongest guarantee an investor can get. Effectively the FDIC insurance has the same backing.

Mutual Funds

Some investors favor mutual funds over many other bank-type investments. With a mutual fund, risk is spread by owning several companies instead of only one. The mutual fund manager may invest in a variety of industries or several companies in the same industry. An investor should analyze mutual funds for risk and objectives. Mutual funds sold by a bank are not insured.

Annuities

Annuities are investments that are underwritten by insurance companies but also sold at other institutions. Annuities are not FDIC insured.

Funds That Are Not Deposits

When purchasing mutual funds, stocks, bonds, or other investment products, at a bank or anywhere else, funds so invested are not deposits and are not insured by the FDIC. Mutual funds are protected against fraud and theft through extensive regulations administered by the Securities and Exchange Commission and state securities regulators.

SIPC INSURANCE

Securities, including mutual funds, held by a broker or a bank's brokerage subsidiary, may be protected by the Securities Investor Protection Corporation (SIPC), a nongovernment entity funded by assessments paid by members. SIPC protects customer accounts against physical loss of their securities up to $500,000, including up to $100,000 in cash, if a member brokerage or bank brokerage subsidiary fails. Securities purchased by a bank for trust accounts or other purposes and held by a SIPC member brokerage or bank brokerage subsidiary also are protected by SIPC.

POSSIBLE CONFUSION

Since both SIPC and the FDIC provide a seal for members to display, and both specify cash limits that look the same, consumers might confuse the two. Only the FDIC protects the money you have in a deposit account. Neither the FDIC nor SIPC protects the money you invest in a nondeposit product such as a mutual fund or other security.

Another important fact about SIPC and FDIC insurance on deposit accounts is that neither insures against loss in the value of an investment account.

STEPS TO BE TAKEN

There is much concern over consumers' not being aware that investments in mutual funds and certain other products are not FDIC insured. The concern has prompted the FDIC and other financial institution regulators to issue a joint statement for banks that sell mutual funds and annuities. This statement details steps that banks and thrifts should take to minimize the possibility of customer confusion about the account insurance.

The steps include:

1. Having banks obtain a signed statement when a customer opens an investment account acknowledging that the customer has received and understands the disclosure
2. Offering investment products for sale in a physical location that is separate from the area where retail deposits are taken.

THE INVESTOR SHOULD KNOW

Mutual funds have the same market risk, no matter where or how they are purchased. Market risk is totally dependent on the daily price fluctuation of the securities held in the mutual fund. If the market goes up, taking with it the prices of the securities in a mutual fund, the price of the mutual fund also goes up. If the market goes down, the price of the mutual fund goes down. If a firm managing a mutual fund goes under, the securities are likely to be covered by SIPC insurance, if the firm is a member.

If a bank fails, only accounts designated as deposit accounts are insured by the FDIC. Each depositor is insured up to $100,000. The FDIC is backed by the United States government.

CHAPTER 26

Buy More Shares with No Commission

The broker calls and says that the growth fund you purchased a couple of months ago is doing well. Further, there is currently a special deal where you can buy more shares with no commission charge. Is it true? How can the broker make any money? It's time to ask for more details.

LESS THAN FORTHRIGHT

More than one broker has been guilty of either not saying anything about sales charges on mutual funds or suggesting that there were no commissions charged on a mutual fund purchase. It was really a game of words. Load mutual funds don't have commissions charged, but they do have that load, also known as a sales charge. Many times, it is not easy to see the sales charge in the account. It's not usually listed separately, unlike stock commissions.

SOMETIMES THERE'S NO CHARGE

Probably because of competition, some load funds converted themselves into no-load funds in the past few years. Investors had the opportunity to add shares to their portfolio with no commissions or sales charges. Additionally, the sale of mutual funds and other securities is a business, and a business has bargains from time to time.

TELL ME ABOUT IT

Ask the broker why there is currently no sales charge on the fund.
Will the sales charge be added later or has the fund become no-
load? This will also let you know if the special deal will be available for awhile.

CHECK FURTHER

Tell the broker you want to think about it and will call back. Call
the office where the broker works and ask to speak to the sales
manager. If he or she is unavailable, ask to talk to a compliance person. Either one should be able to provide further details on the broker's offer.

NOT FREE

Investing is not free. If it were, there wouldn't be any investments.
Any time the words "there's no commission charge" are heard, ask
what other fees are involved. If there are no other fees, ask how the
broker is compensated for the trade.

CHAPTER 27

Mutual Funds Are Automatically Diversified

Suppose you buy stock in just one company. With one company, there is no diversification. If the company does well and the price increases, you make a profit when the stock is sold. If the company does not do well and the price drops, you lose money if the stock is sold. But if you invest in the common stock of two or three companies, gains from one (or more) can offset losses in the others. And if you invest in a hundred companies, any losses could be further offset.

SAFETY IN NUMBERS

Diversification is based on the concept of safety in numbers. The more stocks in the investment portfolio, the less price damage any one stock can cause when its price drops. Furthermore, the chance of having high price performance with some of the companies in the mutual fund is increased.

Even with diversification, though, market risk, the possibility of a sharp correction or bear market, still exists. A mutual fund only provides some protection against market risk, and that protection is dependent on the fund's objective. For example, an aggressive growth fund might be damaged more by a market decline than a conservative growth fund. That's because aggressive growth funds invest in stocks with higher risk than conservative growth funds.

Higher risk can mean greater volatility and drops that are more dramatic when the stock market declines sharply.

DIVERSIFIED BY INDUSTRY AND COMPANY

Many mutual funds have become specialized over the years. Besides being classified by objective as growth or small capitalization, they also tend to diversify by industry and company.

The Franklin Equity Fund (Class A) has existed since January 1, 1933. At the end of 1998, the total net assets of the fund stood at $627,700,000. It's a growth fund, but may also invest in smaller companies or in foreign companies. The fund is diversified by industry as well as company. Table 27-1 shows the industry breakdown for the Franklin Equity Fund as of December 31, 1998.

As of November 30, 1998, the total number of investment positions in the fund was 94. That means an investor putting money into the fund was effectively buying stock in 94 different companies spread through 10 different industries. Some of the larger holdings on November 30, 1998, are listed in Table 27-2.

TABLE 27-1

Franklin Equity Fund Industry Diversification*

Industry	Percent of Portfolio
Financials	14.70
Electronic technology	11.44
Utilities	10.60
Health technology	8.53
Consumer nondurables	7.50
Semiconductors	6.90
Energy minerals	6.14
Technology services	5.61
Transportation	4.32
Industrial services	3.45
Other	11.50
Cash	9.40

*Information from Franklin Templeton, http://www.franklin-templeton.com/.

TABLE 27-2

Top 10 Company Holdings

Company Name	Percent of the Portfolio
Cisco Systems Inc.	3.47
Intel Corp.	2.31
AEX Corp.	1.93
Enron Corp.	1.81
Providian Financial	1.76
Airtouch Communications	1.76
Nokia Corp. (ADR)	1.65
American International Group	1.62
Synopsys Inc.	1.56
Associates First Capital Corp.	1.50

The Franklin Equity Fund has diversification of both industries and companies. Buying shares of the fund will automatically place the investor's money into all the companies in the fund's portfolio of investments.

CHANGES DEPEND ON MANAGERS

Changes in the percentage of assets invested in different industries and in individual companies are up to the investment adviser and portfolio manager of the mutual fund. That is why their length of service in relation to the performance of the fund is often a point of analysis. If a fund has done well for the past 10 years and has had the same manager and investment adviser, that is considered positive. Recent changes in manager or investment adviser are considered by many to be negative events. Logically, analysis of a mutual fund should not be based on the manager's or adviser's tenure alone.

TOO MUCH DIVERSIFICATION

It's possible to have too much diversification. Investing small amounts of money into a multitude of mutual funds, rather than carefully selecting a few with slightly differing objectives, seems pointless. Why have four or five different growth funds?

Spreading investment assets into a well-chosen growth fund, specialty fund, and aggressive growth fund should give the investor good diversification as well as a good opportunity for gains. The funds are well chosen if they show good performance records and fit nicely with an investor's objectives.

CHAPTER 28

The Day's Close Is Very Important

The one consistent quality of the stock market is that it tends to fluctuate daily. Some days it moves only a few points up or down. On other days significant moves can take an investor by surprise. What the market does during a trading day can be very important to the mutual fund investor. No matter what the market does, open-end mutual funds are priced at the end of the day. Prices are checked, and the net asset value of the fund is calculated with any fees deducted. The net asset value is what fund sellers receive if they choose to redeem their shares. If the fund is a load fund, a sales charge is added on to the net asset value to arrive at a *public offering price* (POP), also called a *maximum offering price* (MOP). If the fund is a no-load, the NAV is both the selling and the buying price.

IDEAL DAY TO BUY

What's the ideal day to buy a mutual fund? Obviously, when the market is down for the day. Stock prices tend to move as a group, so if the market is down, chances are a mutual fund candidate is also going to have a lower price.

IDEAL DAY TO SELL

If the ideal day to buy is when the market is down, obviously it's time to sell when the market is up. This advice is not intended to recommend short-term profit taking. Mutual funds should be a long-term investment and should not be sold just because the market or the fund price is up. But when the decision to sell has been made, timing the sell to a strong upward-moving day can add extra dollars to that net asset value.

CHAPTER 29

Are Mutual Funds Transferable?

One of the questions that needs to be answered when investing in a mutual fund through a representative organization (brokerage firm, bank, or insurance firm) is, Can the fund be transferred to another firm? Don't worry about offending someone with this question. The transferability of funds is variable from fund to fund. Some can be transferred and others cannot. Many can be moved electronically from firm to firm by use of an ACATS form.[1] The ACATS system allows the transfer of mutual fund shares between broker-dealers.

A situation can arise where the investor desires to change investment firms. Either the securities can be withdrawn in certificate form and transferred to the new firm, or the new firm can request an account transfer through the ACATS system. Although outstanding debits in an account must be satisfied, they should not interfere with an account transfer.

Investors transfer accounts for many reasons. They can be anything from dissatisfaction due to inadequate service to a simple consolidation of a number of investment accounts into two or possibly three. The investor must complete a form requesting the transfer with the new or receiving firm. The broker then turns

---

1. An account transfer form used by the Automated Customer Account Transfer Service system of the National Securities Clearing Corporation.

the form over to the account transfer department, and the request is processed. The transfer should take only a few days.

EXPEDITIOUSNESS REQUIRED

The National Association of Securities Dealers requires that account transfers between broker-dealers be done expeditiously. To make an account transfer, the new or receiving broker must submit the request to the carrying broker-dealer. According to the NASD, the carrying broker-dealer must respond within three business days. Exemptions must be promptly resolved between the two firms, and the securities must be transferred within four business days of validation of the transfer instructions.[2]

EXCEPTIONS

Some investments are not transferable between firms. Investments that might not be transferable are proprietary products of the carrying broker-dealer or mutual funds (or other assets) where the receiving firm does not maintain the arrangement necessary to hold the asset in the customer's account. Obviously, with more than 6,000 different mutual funds, not every fund is carried by every investment firm.

When investments cannot be transferred, the investor must be offered three choices:

- Liquidate the investment (sell it).
- Keep the investment at the original firm (don't transfer it).
- Have the investment certificate sent out (take physical delivery).

ASK AHEAD OF TIME

Although it is human nature to feel uncomfortable asking about the transferability of mutual funds at the time of investment, it is worthwhile. Finding out at the last minute that some funds cannot

---

2. NASD Uniform Practice Code Rule 11870.

be transferred to a different firm can be irritating and upsetting. In some situations, the possible delay might also be costly. Brokers are frequently asked if the funds they are promoting can be transferred. They should not be offended and should offer a prompt, accurate yes or no.

PROPRIETARY FUNDS

Several brokerage firms offer proprietary mutual funds. They are allowed to do so. They are also allowed to determine if the funds can be transferred to another firm, possibly the competition. Although part of the reason for issuing proprietary mutual funds is undoubtedly to control assets, it also enables the firms to hold down administrative costs. Therefore the investor benefits.

MOST TRANSFERS ARE SMOOTH

The vast majority of account transfers are accomplished quickly and easily through the electronic ACATS system. The investor can help the transaction along by deciding what to do with any securities in the account that cannot be transferred to another firm—sell them, keep them where they are, or take physical delivery.

CHAPTER 30

Money Market Funds Are (Not Exactly) the Same

Before the introduction of money funds, the world of money market investing was unavailable to individuals. Only investors (usually institutional) with $100,000 or more could afford to purchase high-yielding money market debt instruments, such as market rate certificates of deposit (CDs) and commercial paper. It wasn't until 1972 that the first money fund—the Reserve Fund—was established, bringing money markets to individuals. Now, more than 1,300 money funds have been created, with assets totaling more than a trillion dollars.

A SHORT-TERM MUTUAL FUND

Money markets are intended to be a short-term investment. Brokerage firms added them as a temporary parking place for cash until the investor desired to make new investments. The cash earns interest and is immediately available for investments or withdrawal. The accounts usually include checking privileges.

THE $1 NAV

Money market managers seek to provide a stable net asset value of $1 per share, while paying a current level of dividend income. The

$1 net asset value constancy is not a requirement, but investment companies work hard to keep it there.

> "No one can afford to break the buck," says Peter Crane, managing editor of IBC's Money Fund Report, referring to the willingness of fund companies to absorb a money fund's losses to keep its net asset value from falling below $1. "It would damage the industry's reputation, and people might turn to federal deposit accounts instead."[1]

The funds are not insured by the FDIC or any other government agency, but rather they invest primarily in low-risk fixed-income securities. The funds buy loans with maturities ranging from 1 day to 1 year. The average maturity cannot be longer than 90 days. The short maturities nearly eliminate interest rate risk, but retain the risk of lowered dividend payments when interest rates decline.

THE SECURITIES

The Securities and Exchange Commission requires that all taxable money market funds invest a minimum 95 percent of their assets in securities of the highest grade (as rated by major credit rating agencies such as Moody's Investors Services or Standard & Poor's Corp.). Credit risk is nearly nonexistent with U.S. money market funds.

TAXABLE MONEY MARKETS

There are three main kinds of taxable money market funds. Income earned by these funds is normally subject to federal taxes (and possibly state and local taxes).

U.S. Treasury Funds

These funds invest principally in direct U.S. Treasury obligations. The income from U.S. Treasury funds is taxed at the federal level but is free of state taxes.

---

1. Amy Kover, "Show Me the Money—and Forget about the Risk," *Fortune*, March 31, 1997, http://cgi.pathfinder.com/fortune/1997/970331/mut3.html.

U.S. Government Funds

They are funds that invest in obligations of the U.S. Treasury and other government agencies. Sometimes these funds are referred to as "federal" money market funds, referring to the fact that they invest in debt obligations of the federal government.

General-Purpose Funds

These funds invest primarily in the short-term debt of large, high-quality corporations and banks.

TAX-EXEMPT MONEY MARKETS

Municipal money market funds invest in the debt obligations of state and local government agencies. Municipal money market funds pay income that is exempt from federal, and sometimes state and local, income taxes. They are usually called tax-free money market funds.

SIMILAR FEATURES

Many money market funds share similar service features. These include free check writing, exchange privileges into other mutual funds in the same family, monthly dividends, and wire privileges.

COMPARING EXPENSES

Other than some aspects of size and quality, the main difference between money market funds is cost. Expense ratios can be low, at about 0.20 percent ($2 for every $1,000 invested), or high, at 2.00 percent ($20 for every $1,000 invested). Obviously, lower cost means a higher yield for investors.

FEES WAIVED

To attract investors, money market funds will waive the management fee for a time. This obviously increases the yield. When the asset base becomes large enough, one can assume the full management fees will be charged.

MONEY MARKET RATINGS

Credit rating agencies like Standard & Poor's and Moody's do run credit ratings on money market funds. In fact, they do ratings for funds in countries other than the United States.

GENERAL SAFETY

U.S. money market accounts, although they are not insured by the government, are essentially safe investments. Because it fears that investors might return their money to the banks at the first sign of trouble, the industry is quick to protect and assist areas of difficulty.

CHAPTER 31

A Fund of Funds Is More Diversification

If the diversification of a mutual fund is such a great investing idea, why not invest in a fund of mutual funds? It would certainly increase the diversification and could possibly spread the risk, with a combination of higher- and lower-risk funds. This idea of mutual funds that only invest in other mutual funds originated back in the 1960s, and it has come into new focus in the late 1990s. The 80-plus funds of funds have attracted assets of more than $21 billion.

However, many believe this to be too much of a good thing. For one, the investor could find the same stocks in several different funds. That rather blows a hole in the goal of increased diversification. But that's not the only problem. What about the fees?

DOUBLE MANAGEMENT FEES

All mutual funds charge management fees. They couldn't exist without them. It takes staffs of people to move that money around and send out all those statements to the investors. The total fees of funds of funds can run as high as 3 to 5 percent—and that's annually. Individual mutual fund management fees are often below 0.5 percent. Some of the larger fund companies, investing in their own funds, charge a management fee only on the holding fund and not on the individual components.

SOME VALUE ADDED

Obviously, investors get some value for the extra cost.

> Fund-of-funds managers say investors are getting value for that extra cost: asset allocation, fund selection, and fund monitoring—all services that investors otherwise must do themselves or pay someone to do for them. And fund-of-funds managers do have some options not available to individuals. Often they can buy load funds without paying a load, or invest in institutional funds.[1]

As noted, asset allocation, fund selection, and fund monitoring are all advantages. There is also a kind of diversification of portfolio managers, which might provide another advantage. In regard to the statement that portfolio managers "can buy load funds without paying a load, or invest in institutional funds," this might be an advantage. But oftentimes the only difference between retail and institutional funds is the minimum investment required.

CATEGORIES AND PERFORMANCE

The Internet site for the Funds of Funds Association[2] analyzes these products by investment style. The two main categories are asset allocation and single-asset allocation.

Asset Allocation

This category can be further subdivided into conservative, moderate, and growth funds.

Conservative

These funds have a low volatility and an emphasis on capital retention. The group has shown volatility less than 50 percent of the S&P 500 Index.

Average 5-year return: 8.39%[3]

---

1. Jeffrey M. Laderman, "A Bunch of Funds Rolled into One," *BusinessWeek*, 1997, http://www.businessweek.com/1997/39/b3546090.htm.
2. http:/www.fundsoffunds.org/.
3. *Performance data source*: Lipper Analytical Services, Inc., period ending March 31, 1999.

Moderate

Moderate funds work for a balance between low volatility and total return. The group has shown 50 to 70 percent of the volatility of the S&P 500 Index. At times, the difference in volatility might be less than and other times greater than the S&P Index.

Average 5-year return: 14.40%

Growth

Growth funds are aggressive funds that tend to target total return without concern for short-term volatility. The group has shown volatility between 70 and 100 percent of the S&P 500 Index volatility.

Average 5-year return: 15.87%

Single-Asset Allocation

Minimums of 65 percent of the held mutual funds are in the same class.

Categories

International	1-year average	−1.94%
Fixed income	5-year average	6.94%
Small company	1-year average	−8.86%

MEDIOCRITY IN NUMBERS

Although many funds of funds don't have a long-term history, it's difficult to get excited about the performance they show. Logically, diversification eventually reaches a point of diminishing returns and leads to mediocrity. Lower volatility than the Standard & Poor's 500 Index is fine to a point, but it can also mean lower performance. Most investors don't mind volatility, as long as it's on the upside. It's the steep, money-losing declines they want to avoid. Most funds of funds haven't experienced an extended bear market, and so no one is certain what will happen when one occurs.

AUTOMATIC ASSET ALLOCATION

For those who like the concept of risk moderation provided by asset allocation, funds of funds can provide an easy alternative. However, the investor must also be willing to accept the possibility of higher fees and oftentimes moderate performance.

A fund of funds could end up to be an index fund, though probably not by intention. That is not necessarily bad, but it's likely easier and less expensive to just buy an index fund. Investment firms tend to create products they can sell. So what's next? Perhaps a fund of funds of funds?

CHAPTER 32

Do Real Estate with a REIT Fund

The best advice my father ever gave me was "buy land, they ain't makin any more of it...."

Will Rogers

A real estate investment trust called a REIT and pronounced "reet" is a company that buys, develops, manages, and sells real estate. REITs enable the investor to buy shares in a professionally managed portfolio of real estate properties. Although their shares trade on stock exchanges, REITS qualify as pass-through entities. They are companies that distribute a majority of income cash flows to investors, without being taxed at the corporate level.

As pass-through entities, REITs normally generate income from property rentals. A major advantage of a REIT is its liquidity. It's easy to buy and sell, compared with actual real estate ownership. Shares of real estate investment trusts trade on the major stock exchanges.

INCOME AND GROWTH

REIT investment grew significantly during the 1980s after the elimination of certain real estate tax shelters. These investments in real estate provided investors with income and price growth. The Tax Reform Act of 1986 allowed REITs to manage their properties directly, and in 1993, barriers to investments by pension funds were eliminated. The trend of reforms continued to increase the interest in REIT investment.

RECENT GROWTH

More recently, REITs have seen extensive growth. They now own approximately 8.3 percent of the $1.3 trillion commercial real estate market. In 1999, more than 300 publicly traded REITs operated in the United States, the average daily dollar volume of which has grown to more than $260 million.

WHO OWNS REITS?

REITs are owned by individual as well as large institutional investors. Institutional investors include pension funds, endo ment funds, insurance companies, bank trust departments, and mutual funds. Several of the major mutual fund companies now offer REIT mutual funds as part of their families.

OBJECTIVES

Investment goals for owning REIT shares are the same as for owning many other corporation stocks: current income and long-term price appreciation.

WHERE TO BUY

The majority of shares of mutual funds can be purchased on the major stock exchanges, and orders can be placed through stockbrokers or mutual fund companies. Financial planners and investment advisers can help an investor compare objectives with individual REIT investments. Mutual funds now specialize in REITs, bringing the benefits of diversification to this form of property investing.

THREE TYPES OF REITS

Equity REITs

Equity REITS invest in and buy various properties. Revenues are generated mostly from rental fees.

Mortgage REITs

Mortgage REITs deal in investment and ownership of mortgages. The REITs lend money for mortgages to owners of real estate and can also buy existing mortgages or mortgage-backed securities. The revenues come primarily from interest earned on the mortgage loans.

Hybrid REITs

Hybrid REITs combine the equity and mortgage REITs by investing directly in properties and mortgages.

SPECIALIZED-AREA INVESTING

REITs can also specialize in certain niche areas. They might focus geographically by region, state, or possibly metropolitan area, or they might concentrate on property types, such as retail properties, industrial facilities, office buildings, apartments, or, sometimes, health-care facilities. Some REITs choose a broader focus by investing in a variety of properties and mortgage assets across a wide spectrum of locations.

PERFORMANCE

The performance of REITs began to track the performance of the stock market at the end of 1994. Institutional as well as individual investors obviously began to find them more attractive. A comparison of the total returns All REITs Index[1] and the Standard & Poor's 500 Index shows a similar trend (Figure 32-1).

The weakness in 1997 can partly be attributed to the strength of the stock market. Undoubtedly, institutional investors sold off REITs and bought corporate stock to partake of anticipated stronger gains. Institutional investors tend to prefer gains over income.

REITS ARE INCOME AND GROWTH

Comparing the All REITs (equity, mortgage, and hybrid) total return index with the Standard & Poor's 500 Index isn't entirely fair. Granted, the S&P Index is used as a benchmark for many portfolios, but these are growth stocks with low dividends. The

---

1. *Data Source:* National Association of Real Estate Investment Trusts, http://www.nareit.com/.

FIGURE 32-1

Total Return All REITs Performance and S&P 500 Index,
March 1994–1999.

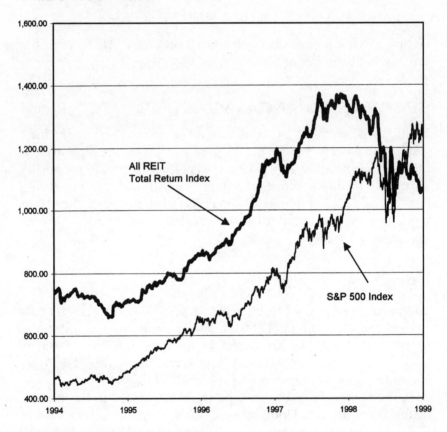

average dividend on the S&P Index was about 2 percent in 1999,
whereas the average dividend for REITs was nearly 8 percent. The
twofold objective of REITs is income and growth.

WEAKNESS OF REIT PERFORMANCE

One of the weaknesses of REIT performance will always be the
fickle strategies of the institutional investor. As the corporate stock
market shows great strength, REITs become less attractive to many

institutional managers. The selling causes REIT prices to weaken, but pushes the dividend yields higher.

REITS, INCOME WITH AN INFLATION HEDGE

The long-term performance of a REIT is determined by the value of its real estate assets. An incentive for REIT investment is the low correlation of its value to that of other financial assets. REITs have low historical volatility and provide some degree of inflation protection, as property prices tend to rise with inflation. Another factor attractive to the investor is that a REIT's performance is monitored on a regular basis by analysts, auditors, and the business and financial media.

Still, the price performance of REITs depends on the price performance of underlying properties, and as Will Rogers's father said: "...they ain't makin any more of it."

CHAPTER 33

It's Best to Invest in Mutual Funds Long Term

Well, of course, it's best to invest with a long-term perspective in mind. That's the only proven way to make any money in the stock market. Brokers who do their job properly remind every investor that mutual fund investing should be a long-term commitment. Select the mutual funds carefully and hang on. If the prices go down, buy more. That might not be the best strategy with an individual stock since it might cease to exist. However, the strategy can be excellent with a mutual fund. The fund has diversification, whereas the individual stock does not.

FUND PERFORMANCE

Mutual fund performance is often measured by either top performance, where it's compared with other funds, or individual performance over a period of time (1, 3, 5, 10 years). Top performance, such as the top 10 mutual funds, can be interesting if the same funds continue to be the top and their reason for being there is relatively transparent. However, a top-performance measure can also be misleading. Those at the bottom one year might be at the top the following year.

Individual performance over a 5- or 10-year period of time might be misleading, because the performance might have been strongest in the beginning of the period. However, most funds also include annual performance, allowing the investor to see where the peak performance occurred. This type of performance is important, as it includes any dividend payments as if they were reinvested, thereby presenting a total return picture.

OLDEST MUTUAL FUND

The fund claiming to be the oldest mutual fund is the Massachusetts Investors Trust (MIT), managed by the MFS Investment Management Company. Founded in 1924, the fund is advertised as being "America's first mutual fund." Although it could be interesting to see how the fund performed in the crash of 1929, the information is not readily available, and it would not be relevant to the current market, anyway. What is readily available is the performance for the past 5- and 10-year periods (Figure 33-1).

10 YEARS AGO

Although the price growth is impressive, what about those who bought the fund back in 1989? How many bailed out because of a lack of performance? Those who bought in October 1989 were probably not too happy in March 1990. The price of the fund had gone nowhere, and then it went down. It was a time for patience.

Those who made a comparison with the rest of the market (Figure 33-1) probably increased their shares by buying more. They could see the problem was the market, not fund performance.

OBJECTIVE

The stated objective of the Massachusetts Investors Trust is "long-term growth of capital and income, and reasonable current income." The portfolio is 95 percent invested in stocks and nothing in bonds, so it is really a growth fund. The emphasis on income in the objective indicates the presence of dividend-paying stocks. That means it is a conservative fund, investing primarily in larger, well-established companies like IBM, General Electric, American Home Products, Microsoft, and Pfizer. Table 33-1 shows the fund's annual compound performance.

FIGURE 33-1

Long Term, 5 to 10 Years.

As you can see from Table 33-1, the compound performance for 1, 5, and 10 years is impressive and would make any conservative investor happy. But would the investor have been happy during the 10-year period?

If the temptation to sell became great enough in the early 1990s, think how unhappy the investors would have been by 1995 or 1998. That's why long-term holding is recommended. The stock market has a buying bias. If it didn't, there would be no stock market.

The chart (Figure 33-2) reveals some consistency in showing a larger increase than the Standard & Poor's 500 Index during the

TABLE 33-1

Annual Compound Performance*

1 year	15.88%
5 years	21.52%
10 years/life	18.45%

*SEC average annual compound rate of
return through December 31, 1998, includes
sales charge and assumes reinvestment of
dividends and capital gains. See the prospectus for full details. www.mfs.com/.
Source: MFS.

FIGURE 33-2

MIT Fund Percent Increase in the Net Asset Value.

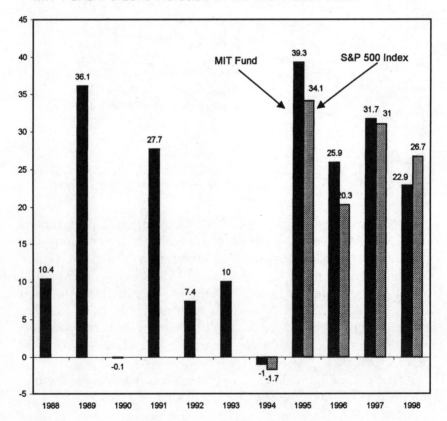

past few years (1994–1997). Only the 1998 percent increase was a bit lower, with a 22.9 percent increase in the MIT Fund and a 26.7 percent increase in the S&P 500. Missing the benchmark S&P 500 could be important if it becomes consistent.

LONG-TERM FOCUS

Although the market has volatility, it's difficult to trade that volatility with stocks. Logically it should be even more difficult to trade that volatility with mutual funds. They were designed as a long-term investment. Being patient and staying with a fund during times that are more difficult (possibly buying additional shares) can be the way to get the most from a mutual fund.

CHAPTER 34

Select a Good Fund for You

There is no such thing as the *best* mutual fund. Trying to find the best is like trying to buy at a market bottom and sell at the top. Even finding the best fund for your personal financial situation could be too labor and time intensive. There are more than 8,000 mutual funds, and the number appears to increase daily. The market could be up another 1,000 points on the Dow Industrial Average before a buy decision is reached. Although many people want to invest, they are much too busy to take on investing as a second job. Doing a small amount of analysis and planning will usually place the investor in a fund with consistent performance, an acceptable objective, and reasonable risk.

FORGET THE TOP PERFORMERS

Maybe not altogether; but top performance can mean many different things, including higher risk. One could argue that the list of top performers will change nearly every day, because each day looks at a different data time frame. In that situation, the top performers of today will be different from the top performers of tomorrow. Also, remember those managers continually fighting for top performance can often end up on thin ice, eventually falling through. Consistent portfolio management can also be an important selection criterion.

Many times, average "ain't too bad." A sum of $10,000 invested in an average domestic stock fund in 1980 would have grown to $90,940[1] during the 15 years that followed. The average gain on the investment would have been 14.8 percent annually. Considering the decline in interest rates and bond yields in that same time period, most would find the gain quite acceptable.

FIRST SET SOME OBJECTIVES

Is income, total return, growth, or speculation the main area of interest? What is the money being invested for: education, a house, retirement, or something else? Make a list of some general objectives (see Chapter 18). Add a few specific details, like how much annual growth is desired (be reasonable). Then set out to find some fund candidates.

INVESTOR OBJECTIVE

To save for retirement, invest $10,000 initially in a growth stock fund, adding $500 more every 3 months. The fund should invest primarily in medium to large companies in the United States. Annual performance should match or exceed the fund's 5-year average annual increase. In years when the market is down, fund performance should be comparable to that of the Standard & Poor's 500 Index.

Although the S&P 500 Index can be used as a reference for the main market performance, it is not an ideal benchmark for every fund. Many funds will make a comparison with a specific index in their literature. That index can be used in place of the S&P 500 Index. Another way to set a standard is to say that fund annual performance should be in the top 30 percent when compared with funds with similar investment objectives.

LOOK TO THE INTERNET

It's difficult to avoid information about mutual funds on the Internet. Investment companies are going to great lengths to pro-

---

1. Based on the 14.8 percent annual average return of all U.S. equity funds.

vide fund investment information to individuals. Using a search engine with the keywords *mutual funds* will bring a large number of site hits. Finding a site that lists mutual fund families can be a timesaving idea. Once found, do a bookmark or list the site in "favorites." The links should provide information on the fund families, individual funds, performance data, and other useful information. Many provide the actual fund prospectus online. Print out the prospectus and other interesting fund information. Much of the information can also be saved to the computer hard drive, but it's usually easier to make comparisons using hard copy.

PEER COMPARISON

The comparison of funds should start with the fund's objectives, strategies, and risk statements (if available). Before looking at performance, be certain to have funds that are trying to accomplish similar goals. It's not fair and could be misleading to compare a precious metals fund with a growth and income fund, for the purpose of selection. If an index fund is comparing itself with the Russell 2000, it really doesn't relate to the Standard & Poor's 500 Index. However, the comparison could be valid to show how growth compares between smaller and larger companies. General comparisons between funds or indexes can help an investor better understand the effectiveness of different strategies.

Compare income funds with income funds, growth funds with growth funds, total return with total return, and speculative with speculative. Keep in mind that the term *growth and income* will often appear instead of the term *total return*. The terms *speculative* or *speculation* will probably never be seen as a mutual fund objective. Instead, the words *high yield* or *aggressive growth* will be used. And although funds will often describe some of the investment risks involved, the word *risk* is usually avoided in the name and objective.

PERFORMANCE

Well, yes, performance is important. Every investor wants a good return on investment. Although past performance is not a guarantee of future results, it's all we have to look at in terms of what the fund has accomplished.

LOOKING AT THE PERFORMANCE OF THREE GROWTH FUNDS

Below are the objective statements for three growth funds. Table 34-1 presents the funds' average annual returns as of December 31, 1998.

Fund A. Seeks growth of capital by investing primarily in common stocks issued by established companies with potential for long-term gains

Fund B. Seeks long-term growth through a highly selective portfolio of medium- to large-sized companies with prospects for maintaining above-average growth, superior financial strength, and distinct competitive advantages

Fund C. Seeks long-term growth of capital

The three funds look like good performers, with the possible exception of Fund A. The figures for Fund A are slightly inflated, because they do not take the sales load into account. The only suggestion in the objective statement that growth might be slower is the phrase "established companies." Established companies often tend to be slower growth than newer companies; however, estab-

TABLE 34-1

Average Annual Returns (December 31, 1998)

Fund Name	1 year, %	3 years, %	5 years, %	10 years, %	Since Inception, %
Fund A*	14.22	15.78	14.01	15.88	12.98 (4/4/66)
Fund B†	31.60	N/A	26.30	N/A	19.90 (5/15/91)
Fund C†	39.98	30.49	26.16	21.20	14.24 (1/6/59)
S&P 500 Index	28.58	28.23	24.06	19.21	N/A

*Not adjusted for sales charge.
†No-load funds.

lished companies also tend to have more price stability and are better able to recover from corrections.

Fund B and Fund C look to be the strongest in terms of growth, and that's what we are looking for here. Take a look at how the growth appeared in each of the years (Figure 34-1). Since Fund B started in the middle of 1991, its performance on the chart begins with its first full year of operation in 1992.

The only strong year for Fund A was back in 1991. In fact, this can be an argument against picking a top performer based on 1-year analysis. Look at what happened the following year. Those

FIGURE 34-1

Yearly Percent Increase for Funds A, B, and C.

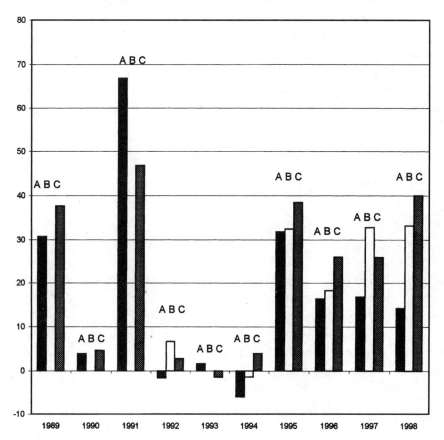

who bought the fund at the end of 1991 were probably not very happy. It's likely that a number of disenchanted investors bailed out of the fund in the next couple of years.

As Figure 34-1 illustrates, 1992 through 1994 were not kind years to any of these funds. It wasn't until 1995 that the stock market took off again. All three funds showed great improvement, but Fund A lagged behind Funds B and C. It's difficult to come up with a reason for the lower performance of Fund A. Possibly, the objective is stated in terms that are too general. The additional information suggests that the fund is a value fund rather than growth. Since we're looking for a growth fund, Fund A is easily eliminated for performance and objective. For the future, Fund A, with its value approach, could still be a good fund, but for now it's not what we're looking for here.

Looking at specific years gives a better picture of the 1-year, 3-year, 5-year, and 10-year performance figures. One fund could have the strong performance at the beginning of the time period and be running out of steam. Two funds can look virtually the same. But when the individual-year performances are viewed, it presents a different picture. We still have Funds B and C in the comparison.

Risk Statement (Main Points)

Fund B

Main risks
- The fund's returns and net asset value will go up and down.
- Market movements will affect the fund's share prices on a daily basis.
- Declines are possible both in the overall stock market and in the types of securities held by the fund.
- The portfolio management team's skill in choosing investments will determine the fund's ability to achieve its objective. The market value of the fund will fluctuate, and the investor could lose money.

Fund C

Market risk.   The fund's return will fluctuate as the stock market cycles.

Manager risk. Poor stock selection could cause the fund to underperform.

Objective risk. Large-capitalization growth stocks can perform better or worse than small-capitalization stocks or growth stocks. There could be times when the large-capitalization stocks fall behind the rest of the market.

Concentration risk. The fund's holdings are at times concentrated in a few industrial sectors. This can cause less diversification and sometimes cause the fund to underperform the market.

Most of the risk statements paraphrased here are generic. They are statements that make the investor aware of the possibility of losing money. The only point of interest is the concentration risk in Fund C. It could easily mean the risk could be greater with this fund.

PERFORMANCE AND MARKET

Both Funds B and C compare their performance with the Standard & Poor's 500 Index, so a daily comparison of the three can illustrate what happens in lousy markets. They are not index funds, but the performance patterns should be similar (Figure 34-2).

On the chart (Figure 34-2), we see a distinct similarity between the three price trend lines. The three have a strong tendency to move in concert, with Fund C being only slightly more volatile. Essentially, when the market moves up, Funds B and C move up. Corrections in the fund appear to line up with corrections in the market.

CONSISTENT INVESTMENT STRATEGY

The fund being selected is for growth, more specifically, large U.S. company growth. This might later be balanced against a smaller-capitalization fund, but for the fund selected here it's important to have a consistent strategy. We don't want this fund to follow each hot successive sector.

A mutual fund analysis company called Morningstar classifies mutual funds by investment style or focus, as well as market capitalization. Morningstar classifies both of these funds as

FIGURE 34-2

Fund B and Fund C Price (NAV) Tracking.

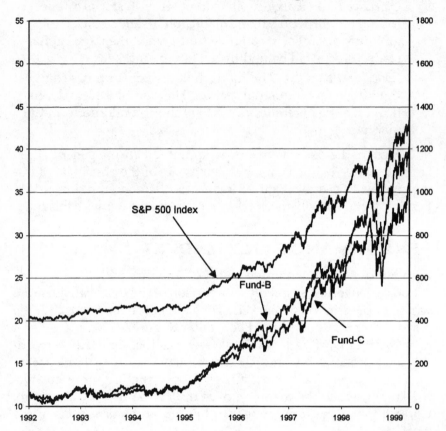

large-capitalization growth funds. Morningstar information also shows past styles for funds that have had changes. The quick and easy way to check investment style is to look at the style boxes used by Morningstar. The mutual funds will usually show the style boxes in their literature.

CHECK THE SECTOR DIVERSIFICATION

Does the fund diversify among industry sectors, or does it concentrate in one area? Some funds will shift assets heavily into something hot like the technology sector and get hit extra hard when the sector falters. The information presented by the fund should show its sector diversification. Some will even compare that diversification with the previous year's. Table 34-2 shows sector diversification for Funds B and C.

As the table shows, the largest differences are in the manufacturing sector, with Fund B at 9 percent (C is at 2 percent), and the financial sector, with Fund C at 12 percent (B is at 7 percent). There is diversification here, but it's also easy to see the concentration in the technology, health, and consumer (discretionary and staples) sectors. The concentration gives the funds increased depth in higher-growth sectors. The depth strengthens performance at the cost of increasing the risk. Being in these top four areas does provide diversification with only a moderate increase in risk. Although funds with lower risk could be found, they also would likely have lower performance.

FUND MANAGEMENT

What is the tenure of the portfolio managers? Although many say that change in management is a reason to sell out of a mutual fund,

TABLE 34-2

Sector Diversification

Sector	Fund B	Fund C
Technology	21%	25%
Health	19%	23%
Consumer discretionary	14%	12%
Consumer staples	14%	16%
Manufacturing	9%	2%
Financial	7%	12%
Durables (consumer)	6%	2%
Durables (other)	4%	N/A
Service industries	4%	
Communications	2%	
Other		8%

it's not necessarily so. If the investor buys a mutual fund one year and the following year a new manager takes over, it's not necessarily a reason to get out. What's the background of the new manager? If the person has been a successful manager in charge of other funds in the same investment company, stay with the long-term objective. If the manager has a successful track record with other portfolios, stay with the fund. In all likelihood, by the time an investor learns of new management, it's too late anyway; any damage from the change will have already occurred.

WHAT ARE THE COSTS?

Please notice, cost here is the final consideration, not the first. Using it as the first consideration can eliminate some excellent funds that are well worth some extra cost. All the considerations listed here are more important than cost and that includes sales charges. The debate over load and no-load funds will rage on for some time. Most of the controversy is misleading, and some of it is inaccurate and incorrect. That is why there are still many load funds around.

Objective, strategy, performance, style, consistency, diversification, and portfolio management are easily more important than the cost of the fund selected. However, it's important to be aware of costs; and with two otherwise equal funds, cost becomes part of the selection.

Table 34-3 shows annual costs for Funds B and C.

FUNDS A, B, AND C ARE REAL

The funds used as examples here are real funds from respectable investment companies. The names were omitted so they wouldn't become a factor in the selection process. Similar analysis can be used to select mutual funds to match any objective.

The investor who wants just a bit less volatility would probably select Fund B. Someone not so concerned about volatility would probably be sold by the final puzzle piece—the low management fee in Fund C. At this time either one could be a good selection, a match for the objective established earlier in this chapter.

TABLE 34-3

Fee Description	Fund B	Fund C
Maximum sales charge	None	None
Maximum deferred sales charge	None	None
Maximum charge on reinvested dividends and distributions	None	None
Redemption fee	None	None
Exchange fee	None	None
Annual Operation Expenses (Deducted from Fund Assets)		
Management fee	0.70%	0.38%
Distribution (12-b-1) fees	None	None
Other expenses	0.49%	0.03%
Total annual fund operating expense	1.19%	0.41%

CHAPTER 35

Look to the Internet for Information

The Internet already has some incredible information for investors, and it gets better every day. Many mutual fund families have web pages with information about their company and about investing in general, as well as information and prospectus downloads for their funds.

PROSPECTUS CAUTION

Many funds use one prospectus for several funds and the reader has to be careful to understand which information relates to which fund. It might be best to print out the prospectus or have one mailed out. It's easier to make comparisons with hard copy.

LINKS

Information can be found either by using a search engine and keywords or by going to link pages that will provide many different topics. Bookmarking or saving a link page as a favorite can keep it handy for later referral. Here are some useful links on the Internet.

Regulatory Agencies and Government

Federal Trade Commission
http://www.ftc.gov/
The FTC is an interesting site with much helpful information for consumers. Sometimes, it also has information on how to avoid investment frauds.

The U.S. Securities and Exchange Commission (SEC)
http://www.sec.gov/
The SEC is the main governmental regulatory body for investing in the United States. The site frequently has useful information for investors, including information on mutual funds. Recently the site provided a mutual fund "cost calculator" so investors could calculate sales charges and management fees in terms of investment cost.

The National Association of Securities Dealers (NASD)
http://www.nasd.com/
The NASD is the investment industry's self-regulatory agency. The site has a great deal of useful information for the investor, including information on training, protection, education, brokers, NASDAQ stock quotes and historical data, publications, and other web sites.

Federal Reserve Bank
http://www.stls.frb.org/fred/index.html
The Fed always has interesting information about economics and interest rates. The Federal Reserve Bank of St. Louis has the FRED database, containing historical data on bonds and other fixed-income investments.

Consumer Information Center, Pueblo, Colorado
http://www.pueblo.gsa.gov/
The site has some useful, basic information on saving and investing.

Mutual Fund Information

Most of the link pages listed here contain good amounts of free investor information. The pages have advertisements that pay for their existence. Some Internet Web sites are by registration and others by paid subscription. In addition, some sites are listed which are a combination of free and fee.

Active Investment Research
http://www.stockresearch.com/funds.html
Active Investment Research has an index on the left side of the screen listing such things as no-charge subscription, newsletter (E-mailed), recommendations for buys, investing education, economic updates weekly, U.S. Treasury bond yield curve, comments on investing philosophy, examples of historical results, other data (quotes and graphs), an archive of information, other research information sources, information on financial planning, a list of other Internet Web sites, and a survey.

Also included is a section of articles under the main heading "Mutual Fund Resources," which includes articles of "General Information on Mutual Funds." The articles section is followed by a "Mutual Fund Search and Screening Engine," as well as links to major mutual fund companies and a list of additional search engines for other mutual funds.

Allstocks.com, The Investors Web Site
http://www.allstocks.com
The site has a number of different subjects, which can be referenced with a mouse click. Although it's a bit heavy into stocks, it also covers annuities, insurance, mutual funds, investment books, and stockbrokers.

DailyStocks.com! The web's first and biggest stock research site!
http://www.dailystocks.com/fundlinks.htm
Although the title suggests it's heavy on stocks, the site is also strong on mutual fund information. The site includes information on specific funds, mutual fund news, fund screens, top performers, columns, SEC filings, and other subjects.

Fund$pot
http://www.fundspot.com/main.shtml
Fund$pot has research, news, education, discussions, questions
answered, and shopping to help the mutual fund learn about and
invest in mutual funds.

invest-O-rama
http://www.investorama.com/
  invest-O-rama has a special list of mutual fund departments,
which currently include:

  Fund families

  Fund analysis and research

  Fund software

  Stock and fund screening

  Closed-end funds

  Closed-end fund analysis and research

  Also included are various articles on mutual fund investing.
The current list of articles refers to hot funds, fees, investing mistakes, risk, and Internet funds. Additionally, the site includes stock
quotes, company profiles, today's news, search engines, message
boards, investing books, and a list of other sites.

miningco.com
http://www.mutualfunds.miningco.com/mlibrary.htm
The Mining Company's motto is "we mine the net so you don't
have to." Under its Mutual Funds category it includes:

  Content: with a welcome, netlinks, articles, guide bio, search,
  related

  Community: with boards, chat, events, newsletters, feedback,
  share this site

  Shopping: with books, marketplace, videos, yellow pages

  It also has links to an "ever-evolving index of useful and/or
entertaining Net resources in mutual funds." The links are organized by category and compiled by the guide.

Morningstar
http://www.morningstar.net/
Morningstar analysis is famous for its star rating system, which rates the ability of mutual funds to achieve outstanding growth, considering the risk involved. The system is based on a simple math formula, with the best performers in different categories being ranked. Although the star system is not a performance predictor, many investors rely on it as a part of their selection criteria.

Morningstar has both a free and a premium service on the Internet web site. The free service has several up-to-date articles on mutual funds, stocks, the market, and taxation. Registration is required for part of the free service.

An investor can get quotes, set up a portfolio, read several informative articles, receive investment education, and exchange opinions with other investors. A new regular column, "Women Investing," began in April 1999.

An excellent frequently asked questions section in the Infodesk informs the investor of many of the details of Morningstar's service and products. Morningstar's fund screening system allows the investor to look through more than 6,500 mutual funds, based on specified criteria. It's available at no charge.

The premium service has two membership options: $9.95 per month or $99 for 12 months. Both options have a two-week free trial. Premium membership allows more extensive portfolio analysis. It also sends the investor E-mail reports regarding market developments that could affect portfolios. Breaking market news is also sent to premium members by e-mail.

BE CAREFUL

It's important to be careful on the Internet. Regulatory agencies have much concern about the amount of fraudulent investment schemes that appear and disappear. More than one person has made use of Ponzi's ideas in the past few years. The bad news is, the scheme still works. *Always* get information before you invest and cross-check—verify that the investment is legitimate. Some of the link sites listed here can help you do that.

Also, criticism has appeared regarding the reliability of data sources. These are just some of the reasons an investor should never depend on only one source of information on the Internet. Make a list of several helpful sites and bookmark them or add them to the favorites file.

CHAPTER 36

Buy Funds on the Dips

There are several important principles to keep in mind. The stock market fluctuates. It virtually never moves in a straight line. And stock prices move as a group. As anticipation wavers based on economic developments or announcements, the stock market moves accordingly. Although beginning in 1929 the market stayed down for 4 years and much later beginning in 1977 it stayed down for 5 years, most market declines are more short term. Many bear markets last only 4 to 6 months.

> For 10 straight years, every time the stock market has taken a hit, you've made big money if you jumped in with both feet. A "buy the dips" philosophy has outperformed any other strategy imaginable.[1]

James Cramer, a renowned hedge fund manager on Wall Street, goes on to say how the one exception to this was the market crash of 1987. However, the biggest difference between then and the 1990s is the fact that interest rates were rising in 1987.

---

1. James J. Cramer, "Stick with the Dips Crash or Not, Buying after a Drop Still Makes Sense," *Business,* vol. 150, no. 16, October 20, 1997, http://www.pathfinder.com/time/magazine/1997/dom/971020/business.stick_with _th.html.

INDEX AND GROWTH FUND COMPARISON

Comparing the Standard & Poor's 500 Index and the Vanguard US Growth Fund for the past 5 years shows the validity of buying on the dips in this market (Figure 36-1). The Vanguard fund is a relatively large fund at $9.59 billion strong (August 1998), and its prospectus says it is for "relatively aggressive" investors looking for long-term growth.

The Standard & Poor's 500 Index is representative of the stock market, and the Vanguard US Growth Fund is representative of

FIGURE 36-1

Vanguard US Growth Fund and S&P 500 Index, 1994–1999.

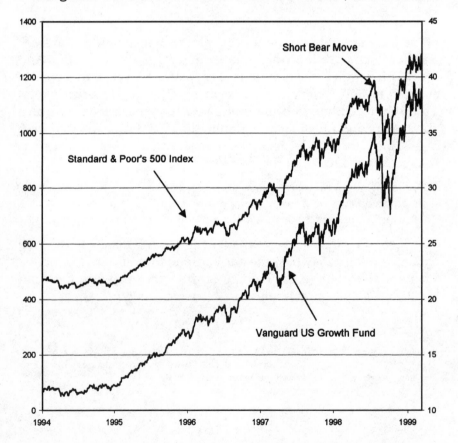

some of the larger growth funds. Although the representation might not be perfect, it will suffice for a look at market dips.

NOT LOOKING AT PERFORMANCE

Although mutual fund investors are always looking for good performance, the purpose of this comparison is to see how well an investor would have fared buying on the dips during the 1994–1999 (March) period. The illustration here is not to show performance.

An important fact to remember is that during the years 1995–1999 investors could virtually do no wrong. The market took off in late 1994 and wouldn't let anything stop its upward progress. But even the strongest markets have spots of weakness. Weakness in a bull market, where there is pressure to keep interest rates down, creates investment opportunities.

OPPORTUNITY FOR LONG-TERM INVESTORS

Probably during every bull move since the late seventies, so-called experts claimed the move unusual—as if to say, once this bull market is over, it will drop and go back to the slow market it used to be. Probably those same experts say the market should always stay with its 12 percent annual average growth. Fortunately, the market doesn't depend on experts. Rather it relies on buyers and sellers to determine strength and direction.

Dips are good for both short-term stock traders and long-term mutual fund investors. Temporary price weakness, caused by market weakness, can provide excellent opportunities to build a portfolio position. The situation allows the investor to buy mutual funds on sale.

CHAPTER 37

A Hedge Fund Is
a Different Animal

As noted in an earlier chapter, one of the earliest known forms of group investing was the "pool," sometimes called the "blind pool." The pool was usually composed of wealthy individuals who put their money together and hired an investment manager to do the investing for them. Managers who had large pools under their control had tremendous financial power. They could influence the price movement of a company to their personal advantage. For example, they could run a stock price up using pool money, but sell short for a personal account. When the price rose high enough, they would sell stocks in the pool and close out the short position when the prices dropped.

WHAT IS A HEDGE?

In finance, a hedge is a counterinvestment taken to offer some protection for the main investment strategy. Investment hedges are specifically used to lower risk. To "hedge a bet" is to take countermeasures to lower risk on a wager.

Although the word carries an implication of measures being taken to lower the investment risk, many hedge funds don't take such measures. In fact, quite the opposite. Hedge funds frequently choose higher-risk investments that have the potential for higher rewards. The term *hedge* is a misnomer with these funds. A hedge fund now is any type of private investment partnership.

HEDGE FUND

A hedge fund is a private investment. It is not publicly traded on or off any exchanges. Effectively it is a limited partnership investing in a variety of securities. Hedge funds have a general partner and limited partners.

The individual or organization that originated the hedge fund is the general partner. The general partner handles all the trading activity as well as the day-to-day operations of running a fund. The limited partners supply most of the money as an investment but do not participate in running the fund. These are pooled investments. All the partners' money is pooled together for the purpose of trading in securities. The funds follow a trading strategy. Normally, they are allowed to use any financial instrument they wish.

BORROWED MONEY

Many hedge funds utilize leverage at an average of 2:1. In a few cases, hedge funds exceed the 2:1 ratio, and that adds to the risk. Borrowed money for investing (margin loan) enables the investor to buy more securities. When the market favors the investment, the investor reaps the profits and pays back only the loan amount. If the market is unfavorable to the investment, the loan amount stays the same and must be paid back.

> Hedge funds, aimed at wealthy individuals or institutions to pursue a variety of investing strategies, have become increasingly popular. Despite their name, many of these funds involve substantial risk because they borrow money to leverage their investments. If those investments prove ill-fated, whether they are in Russian bonds or technology stocks, the losses can be sizable.[1]

FEES

Hedge fund managers are rewarded for performance. If the fund makes money, the managers do well. If the fund is flat or loses money, the managers receive little or no compensation. As set forth

---

1. "Hedge Funds Take Beating," *San Jose Mercury News,* September 3, 1998, originally from the *New York Times.*

in the partnership agreement, the manager's incentive fee is often 20 percent of the net profits. An annual administrative fee, ordinarily 1 percent of the net asset value, is charged by the general partner. Remaining profits or losses are divided among the partners according to their ownership percentage. In the right markets, hedge fund managers can make big money.

IT'S A SECRET

Hedge funds are not allowed to advertise. Not advertising is part of the limited partnership agreement allowing them to avoid some SEC regulations. Therefore little information about them is available. The funds accumulate money for investment through consultants or referrals from current investors. Many managers take customers with them as they leave the employment of large Wall Street firms.

NOT FOR THE $1,000 FLYER

Many individual investors have neither the assets nor the minimum financial base to invest in hedge funds. Funds are required to qualify customers by net worth and income suitability. Minimum investment requirements tend to be considerably higher than they are for mutual funds and unit trusts. As hedge funds are private investment partnerships, the SEC limits hedge funds to 100 investors, at least 65 of whom must be "accredited."

> To be accredited one must have a net worth (including one's home and furnishings) in excess of $1,000,000 or has had an individual income of more than $200,000 for the past two years or joint income with one's spouse in excess of $300,000 in each of these years and has a reasonable expectation to reach the same income level in the current year.[2]

A VARIETY OF TYPES[3]

Hedge funds can be formed with any number of different strategies. Here is a list of some common types:

---

2. George P. Van, chairman, "Quantitative Analysis of Hedge Fund Return/Risk Characteristics," Van Hedge Fund Advisors, Inc., 1998, http://www.vanhedge.com/bookchpt.html.
3. Based on information from Van Hedge Fund Advisors, Inc., 1997.

Aggressive Growth (small stocks); Distressed Securities (turn-arounds); Emerging Markets (non-U.S.); Financial Services (financial institutions); Fund of Funds (other hedge funds); Healthcare, Income (current income); Macro (global investing); Market Neutral-Arbitrage/Convertible Arbitrage (works price differences); Market Neutral-Securities Hedging (long and short stock positions); Market Timing; Media-Communications; Opportunistic (changing strategies); Several Strategies (predetermined strategies); Short Selling, Special Situations (long or short "event-driven" by bad or good news); Technology; Value (undervalued companies).

Several Strategies

The manager employs several specific, predetermined strategies in an effort to diversify an approach to the market. The manager might use a value, aggressive growth, and special situations strategy in the same fund. The objective of such an approach could be to realize short- and long-term capital gains.

FUND PERFORMANCE

How well do hedge funds perform? It probably depends on who is asked and when. According to Van Hedge Fund Advisors International, a company that tracks over 1,500 hedge funds, they do quite well.

HEDGE FUNDS VERSUS MUTUAL FUNDS

Table 37-1 compares the net compound annual returns for a 5-year period, from 1993 (fourth quarter) to 1998 (third quarter). Although this comparison only looks at the top performing hedge and mutual funds, the differences are significant. To have an extra 3.7 percent or 7.0 percent over an already top-ranking return could be very pleasant to investors.

NOT ALWAYS GREAT

The markets are not always kind to hedge funds. These funds have bad times as well as good. In at least part of 1998, they had some performance difficulties. A *Wall Street Journal* article notes:

TABLE 37-1

Net Compound Annual Returns, 1993–1998

Group	Hedge Funds, %	Mutual Funds, %	Hedge Advantage, %
Top 10 performers	29.4	25.7	3.7
Top 10 percent	25.4	18.4	7.0
Top 25 percent	21.4	15.9	5.5

Emerging markets hedge funds plummeted 10% in September and are down a hefty 45.6% for the year, according to Van Hedge Fund Advisors, a Nashville, Tennessee, fund-tracking firm. Chicago-based Hedge Fund Research, or HFR, estimates emerging markets hedge funds fell 4.78% in September and are off 34.68% so far this year.[4]

According to the article, emerging markets had the most difficult time (−23.95 percent) in September 1998, but it wasn't the only type of hedge fund with a bad month. Other negative returns in September occurred with:

Distressed securities	−3.0%
Global macro funds	−3.2%
Market-neutral equity funds	−1.3%
Short sellers	−7.5%

Still, although these categories were having some difficult times, the Van U.S. Hedge Fund Index was actually up 1 percent in September, after being down 6 percent in July.

RISK REWARD

It must be remembered that higher rewards usually mean higher risk. Higher risk means the investor can lose money. Although hedge funds provide an additional investment avenue, many are highly speculative and have considerable risk.

4. Staff reporters Pui-Wing Tam, Laurie Lande, and Sara Calian, and Margaret Boitano of Dow Jones Newswires, "Emerging Markets Plague Hedge Funds," *Wall Street Journal Europe,* October 23–24, 1998.

Buy Funds Cheaper with Dollar Cost Averaging

Buy mutual funds where the average cost per share is less than the average share price. How can this be done? By purchasing a larger number of shares when the price of the shares is lower and fewer shares when prices are higher.

IT'S A DISCIPLINE

Dollar cost averaging is the discipline of setting a regular, long-term investment program for a portfolio, in terms of a set dollar amount which the investor can afford (e.g., $100, $1,000, or $5,000 invested monthly or quarterly). The periodic investing takes the place of attempting to predict when a stock is at its low or high.

By investing the same amount regularly, say $1,000 every month, the investor will buy more units when fund prices are low and fewer units when prices are high. The strategy results in a portfolio with an average of costs. Obviously, units or shares purchased at a lower price will outperform those bought at the higher price. Since dollar cost averaging is being used, more of the "high-performance units" are bought when prices are low. The system can work with buying actual shares of stock or mutual funds.

MUTUAL FUNDS MORE SUITED

Actually, mutual funds are more suited for dollar cost averaging because they are not bound by round lots (100 shares) or full shares. All the money is invested in the shares of the mutual fund purchased. This also makes it easy to set up an automatic purchase plan with a mutual fund company.

SELECTING A FUND

Select a mutual fund based on personal objectives and risk tolerance. For example purposes here, we select the Scudder Classic Growth Fund.[1] The fund invests in medium-to-large companies in the United States. The companies selected are seasoned and are believed likely to add to their value by earnings growth.

COMPARISON WITH THE S&P 500 INDEX

From the brief description it sounds like the fund might be similar to the Standard & Poor's 500 Index, although it is not promoted as an index fund. A chart of the daily prices along with the S&P 500 Index might prove interesting (Figure 38-1).

From the fund's inception in 1997 to early 1999, it has closely followed the S&P 500 Index. Although it might not always follow the index so closely, it certainly has done so in this bull market, including the 1998 bear move.

A CLOSER LOOK AT PRICE HISTORY

As the prices of stock in a stock mutual fund change, the net asset value changes accordingly. The net asset value is a combination of all prices, less any fund expenses, translated into a price per share. The NAV is calculated at the end of each trading day.

PRICES

Investors who purchased shares when the Scudder Classic Growth Fund began would have paid a price of $13.50 per share. A thousand dollars invested would have purchased 74.074 shares of the fund. It

---

1. As of April 15, 1998, this fund is no longer open to new investors. It is used here only for the purpose of serving as an example.

FIGURE 38-1

Scudder Classic Growth Fund, 1997 to 1999.

is a no-load fund; therefore the buy and sell price are both the NAV. The NAV is the lowest price per share for the time period. The highest price was in January 1999 at $21.72 a share, making a gain of $8.22 per share (see Figure 38-2). That is a total $608.89 gain (61 percent). But that's buying at the beginning, and investors often adopt a wait and see attitude toward new securities. Those who bought in April 1998 didn't do so well, buying at a share cost of $20.25.

BUT WHAT ABOUT DOLLAR COST AVERAGING?

Ah, yes, dollar cost averaging, a system that effectively and automatically cuts back on purchases when the price is high and

FIGURE 38-2

Prices for the Scudder Classic Growth Fund, 1997 to 1999

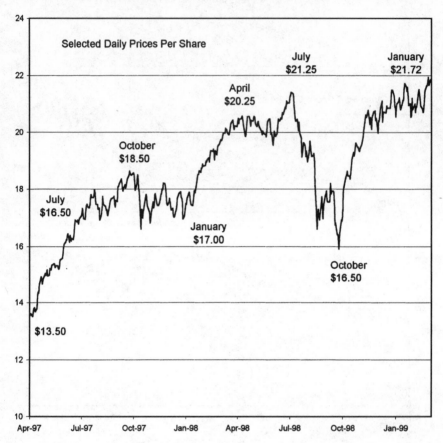

automatically increases the buys when the price is low. It is a system designed to be used by a long-term investor.

Let's say we decide to purchase $1,000 of this fund every 3 months (see Table 38-1). The dollar amount and the buy time remain the same, unless an unusual situation occurs. If the market is dropping, we might want to hold off for a little better price.

The average price for shares drops below the current price with the second purchase. It only rises above the current price once. The one time that the average price per share was above the

TABLE 38-1

Dollar Cost Averaging, $1,000 Invested Every 3 Months

$ Price	Each Buy, Shares	Running Total, Shares	Running Total, Dollars	Average Cost per Share
13.5	74.07407	74.07407	$1,000	$13.50
16.5	60.60606	134.6801	2,000	$14.85
18.5	54.05405	188.7342	3,000	$15.90
17	58.82353	247.5577	4,000	$16.16
20.25	49.38272	296.9404	5,000	$16.84
21.25	47.05882	343.9993	6,000	$17.44
16.5	60.60606	404.6053	7,000	$17.30*
21.5	46.51163	451.1169	8,000	$17.73

*Average price was higher than current price.

going price or current price was during a sharp correction in October 1998. Because the dollar amount remains the same, it buys a greater number of shares when the price is low and fewer shares when the price is high. As you can see from Figure 38-3, the difference is quite dramatic.

The October 1998 instance, where the average price was higher than the current price, is easy to see. The chart in Figure 38-3 clearly shows the advantages of dollar cost averaging. Although waiting in the October situation could have produced a better current price, it would have been difficult to pinpoint when to buy. The market turned quickly and headed for new levels, with this fund being along for the ride.

Periodic investment plans such as dollar cost averaging do not assure a profit or protect against loss in declining markets. The strategy continues to make purchases through periods of low and declining prices. In this way advantage is gained because more shares are purchased at lower prices. The investor still must carefully select the specific investment, whether stocks, bonds, or mutual funds.

FIGURE 38-3

Dollar Cost Averaging.

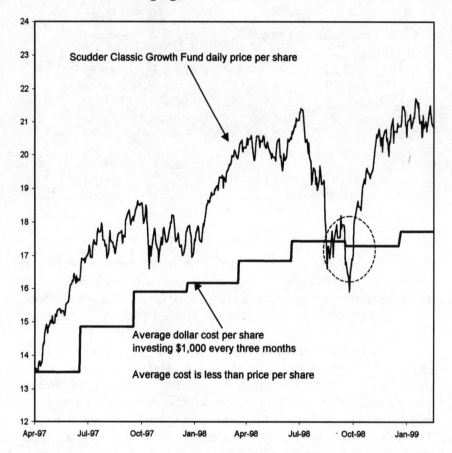

CHAPTER 39

Don't Try to Time the Market (Too Much)

> You can't time the market and make money.
> Time the market one-way only.
> Market timing is a loser's game.
>
> *Anonymous*

So what about this market timing? If the stock market goes up and down, doesn't it make sense to buy when it's down and sell when it's up? It sounds easy. The only problem is deciding how far is down and how high is up. At the turn of the millennium the Dow Industrial Average could easily be down 200 points one day and up 250 the next. It even has the capability of making such a move in a single trading day. The problem with such volatility is estimating the market's direction.

DAY-END PRICING

Open-ended mutual funds calculate prices at the end of the day, which makes it difficult to quickly trade them and take advantage of sudden market moves. They weren't designed to be a short-term, traded security. Mutual funds are designed to be a long-term investment. They take advantage of the stock market's buying bias over time. Trading over the short-term should be left to individual stocks and options.

THE 2000S

Where will the market be in 2005 or 2010? The odds favor it being a lot higher than at the end of the millennium. It won't move straight up. There will be numerous corrections and probably a few bear markets on the way. The economy and the stock market move from crisis to crisis. Sometimes things get tough. Recessions happen and a few companies go out of business; but that's why it's good to invest in mutual funds. The best protection offered by any mutual fund is protection against one or a few companies ceasing to exist.

WHERE IS THE MARKET GOING?

No one knows for certain where the market is going. Even the experts disagree. However, they do tend to agree that the market will continue to rise in the next 10 or more years. Table 39-1 presents a few forecast figures on the Dow Industrial Average.

REASONS TO SELL

1. The money is needed elsewhere or objectives have changed.
2. It's necessary to take a tax loss.
3. There are problems with the fund (performance is low compared with similar funds, problems with operations, changes in the fund that are causing an increase in risk).
4. There is a change in management; or more importantly there is a change in strategy.

Not one of these reasons is related to market swings. If a bear market comes along, add more money, but don't try to pick the bottom. The market can turn in a day and wipe out hundreds of points of Dow Industrial losses.

BUY THE DIPS

Review Chapter 36, "Buy Funds on the Dips." The basic message is buy and buy more, but don't sell unless it is absolutely necessary.

TIMING FUNDS

If an investor truly believes in market timing, some mutual funds will try to avoid the bear moves and take advantage of the bull-

TABLE 39-1

Forecasting the Dow

Forecast	Year	Forecaster	Source
15,000	2005	Ed Yardeni, economist, Deutsche Morgan Grenfell	*Barron's*
18,500	2006	Ralph Acampora, Prudential's chief technician	*Fortune*
21,000	2008	Harry Dent, author of *The Great Boom Ahead*	*Mutual Funds* magazine
21,200	2010	Publisher Sheldon Jacobs	*No-Load Fund Investor*
49,200	2013	(Assuming 15% annual growth)	*Investor's Business Daily*
153,000	2023	Dr. Paul Farrell	*(15% average annual growth, as it has done since 1982)*
400,000	2047	Projection for *Kiplinger's* magazine 100th anniversary*	*Kiplinger's*

*Based on information from Dr. Paul Farrell, "Buy 'n' Hold, and Forget Market Timing, Market Timers Waste Time, Don't Make Money," CBS MarketWatch, March 1, 1999, http://cbs.marketwatch.com/archive/19990301/news/current/superstar.htx?source=htx/http2_mw.

ish advances. But watch out for higher management fees. Also, be aware that buying a mutual fund where professionals do the timing increases the odds of success, but does not guarantee that success.

CHAPTER 40

There's Always a Santa Claus Rally

Santa Claus is comin' to town…and the stock market stages a rally. To the analytical purist, any rally between the Thanksgiving holiday and Christmas Day is a Santa Claus Rally. Actually, nearly every rally in the months of November and December is credited to the "jolly old elf." It's the buying season, a time when some retailers make their year profitable. Consumers go shopping with a frenzy, not just for presents to place under a tree. Many excited shoppers also buy themselves presents.

It's easy to see the Santa Rally for each consecutive year. Each year in Figure 40-1 shows the months of October through December. Probably the most significant rally shown here was the one in December 1994. It began the strongest bull market ever.

1995–1998

By any and all descriptions, this period is the most incredible bull market in history. In the old days, many would have called it the "frenzy at the top" and would have been prepared to sell. The Dow Industrial Average has been like a train, heading for the 10,000-point level (Figure 40-2).

Although the Dow has hesitated at each major 1,000-point level, most hesitations were short-lived. The market stopped to see if anyone wanted to sell and headed upward again. Each year—1995, 1996, 1997, and 1998—showed a small Santa Claus rally, but

FIGURE 40-1

Santa Claus Rally, 1990–1994.

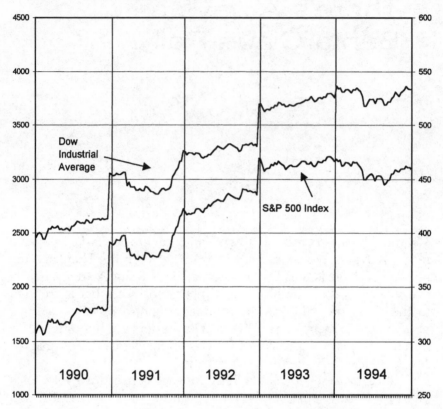

they were minor when compared with the larger bull market rally for each year (see Table 40-1).

The stock market had been fueled by a slow-growth, low-interest-rate, stable economy. Money also flowed into the U.S. stock market from weaker markets around the world, most notably the Asian markets. As the money came in to buy stocks, the prices rose and continued upward.

ALWAYS A SANTA RALLY

On the basis of the past few years, it would seem there will always be a Santa rally, but there's no such thing as "always" in regard to the

FIGURE 40-2

Santa Claus Rally, 1995–1998.

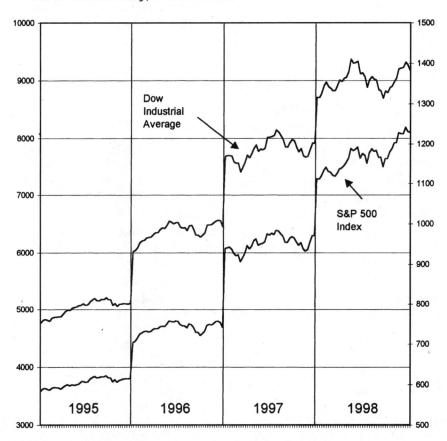

TABLE 40-1

Annual Increases

Year	Dow Industrial Average	Standard & Poor's 500 Index
1995	Up 1282.68 points	Up 156.66 points
1996	Up 1331.15 points	Up 124.81 points
1997	Up 1459.98 points	Up 229.69 points
1998	Up 1273.18 points	Up 258.80 points

fluctuations of the stock market. Because the market trades on antic-ipation of higher or lower prices, it frequently surprises investors with rallies or corrections. Although it is possible to have a bearish trend in the last 2 months of a year, there will likely be some kind of rally. Some rallies are significant, and others are modest.

WHAT DOES THIS MEAN?

To the mutual fund investor, the months of November and December are better times to sell shares than to buy them, unless the market shows an unusually large decline instead of or in addi-tion to the rally.

Buying can somewhat be tied to a year-end sell-off (Chapter 22), but only if the market drops significantly. The general rule, buy on weakness and sell on strength, is true for mutual funds as well as other investments. Selling mutual fund shares on the strength of a Santa Claus rally can provide some extra profit.

CHAPTER 41

Gold Funds as a Hedge

Gold, that rare, yellow, soft metal, has inspired the imaginations of millions of people. For thousands of years, gold has been the commodity that people have relied on to bail them out of difficult times. It is a multiuse commodity, serving as money, jewelry, and an industrial metal, prized for its beauty and properties. Many individuals still believe that when the hard economic times come, gold will remain the only object of value. The belief is based on historic realities.

GOLD PRICES

If we look at the price of gold for the past few years, we can see a certain amount of volatility (Figure 41-1). The price per ounce nearly doubled from 1985 to 1987. It went from $285.75 an ounce to $500. For a 2-year period, that's a significant increase. One would expect to see the price continue rising with that kind of momentum, but it didn't. By 1993 it was back down to $331 an ounce. Then it rose back up, just under $400, and in 1996 fell below $300.

If gold is the currency of choice during times of economic crises, it only stands to reason that the price should experience significant surges if the economy appears to be threatened. In October 1987, the Dow Industrial Average fell a record 507 points in one day. Gold was already high, but it rose another $25 to live up to its

FIGURE 41-1

Gold Prices, 1984–1998.

reputation. However, it didn't keep going. Instead it reversed and began to drop. In late 1998, the record one-day drop for the Dow was broken again, this time by more than 550 points. Gold's reaction was more like a yawn than a rally.

GOLD INVESTORS

Gold investing is done by three types of investors:

Speculators who buy and sell for the fast moves in price

Investors who want to see long-term price growth

Hedgers who buy gold for ongoing inflation protection

The first two (speculators and investors) will stay with gold only as long as they can see results. In February 1996, many of them obviously became disillusioned with gold's glitter and headed for the stock market glory. Their actions had an obvious negative impact on prices.

Although some hedgers will undoubtedly bail out if they don't see significant inflation for several years, many will buy and hold, no matter what happens. They believe that no matter how good things are presently, some day economic troubles will return and gold will regain its shine. Part of their investment portfolio is either directly in gold or in the stocks of gold companies. The price growth of gold companies is based on earnings growth, and that is dependent on the efficiencies of the company as well as the price of gold.

HOARDING PROBLEM

Hoarding is not so much done by individual gold investors as by individual countries, which have had large stockpiles of gold. Whenever they get into financial difficulties or the gold price rises high enough, an activity known as *dishoarding* occurs. A case in point:

> London, May 7 (Bloomberg)—Gold dropped more than 3 percent, its largest one-day decline since 1993, after the U.K. said it will sell more than half its $6.5 billion gold reserves and invest the proceeds in foreign bonds.[1]

As a result of "weak hands" investors who move to the stock market due to a lack of performance with gold, a lack of inflation, and dishoarding, gold can have a difficult time trying to find an accelerating market.

BUY LOW—SELL HIGH

Buy gold now. It's on sale. Buy now at half the price and sell later when the price goes up. Isn't that the whole idea of investing? The

---

1. Bloomberg, L.P., May 7, 1999,
    http://quote.bloomberg.com/news2.cgi?T=news2_ft_topww.ht&s=46484151.

stock market keeps moving to new record highs, making it difficult for the individual investor to climb on the wagon. But gold has been hammered. Does that mean it's time to buy? Some people think so.

"A lot of gold-fund managers are actually bullish on gold," says Amy Granzin, an analyst with Morningstar Inc. "A lot of them are really expecting a rebound."[2]

In 1999, gold had already lost 67 percent of its value since 1980 and was relatively cheap. As a cyclical, the market for it tends to move from cheap to dear. The time to think about gold or gold stock investing is when prices are down. Inflation appeared to be under control, but that could change quickly. Even though the Federal Reserve had become more aggressive in its attempts to head off inflation, its actions have not always been successful.

GOLD OR GOLD FUNDS

Although gold stock and gold mutual funds have additional factors affecting the price, they are generally easier and more convenient vehicles for the individual investor. Gold can be a difficult commodity to deal with when it comes to trading and good delivery. Gold mutual funds are available from most of the major mutual fund families, and most have more than one type of gold fund. Also, closed-end gold funds trade like stock on the exchanges.

It is relatively easy to find gold funds that tend to follow gold prices. They are usually well-established leading funds, like ASA Ltd., which trades on the New York Stock Exchange (NYSE: ASA), and American Century Global Gold mutual fund (BGEIX). American Century Global Gold[3] is one of the larger gold funds, with assets of $326.7 million (Figure 41-2).

Yes, there are differences between gold and gold stock prices. Stock prices, therefore gold mutual funds, are dependent on revenues, earnings, and growth. But the underlying factor is still the price of gold. Other precious metals (e.g., silver and platinum) are

---

2. Timothy Middleton, "New Glitter from Gold Funds," *Mutual Funds*, Microsoft Corporation, 1999.

3. Funds mentioned here are for example only. This is not a recommendation to buy or sell.

FIGURE 41-2

Gold and Gold Funds, 1988–1998.

often included in gold funds. The additions can be considered part of the diversification advantage of fund investing.

HEDGE MIGHT BE BEST

The purpose of a hedge is to moderate loss if the main investment strategy proves incorrect or encounters unexpected reversals. Although gold fund investing has its own set of problems with fickle investors and dishoarding phenomena, the price tends to be low when inflation is low and rises as inflation increases. That can make it a hedge against inflation investment for part of prudent asset allocation.

CHAPTER 42

Never Chase Performance

We want the best, and we don't want to pay too much for it—that's the cry of the American shopper and investor. Competition is a core part of our existence. We want the top athletes, the best companies, the most powerful military, and the top-performance mutual funds. Striving for the best is not all bad, although sometimes it can lead to a situation where we get blind-sided.

WE OFTEN DON'T LISTEN

On every mutual fund prospectus we are told that past performance does not predict future results. Yet whenever a new top list of funds appears in a major publication, the mutual funds are flooded with fresh money.

For many years, the mutual funds industry has told us not to chase after the highfliers, but rather select a fund that best matches our objectives. However, success sells. Just as investors lined up for many blocks to invest their money with Ponzi, we stand in line buying the top mutual funds at constantly increasing prices. The amount of money going into mutual funds sometimes creates buying frenzy, pushing stock prices ever higher. The big get bigger as everyone clamors to get on the bandwagon.

THEN WHAT HAPPENS?

According to a study issued in March 1999 by the Financial Research Company of Boston, our hot investments are often disappointing. The company looked at the lists of the top 10 percent of funds for any 12-month period since 1988. That top group tended to drop to the 48th percentile the following year. Nearly half became below-average performers the following year. On the other side of that coin, 40 percent of the worst-performing funds had above-average gains in the next year.

Call it mutual fund entropy, where funds follow a progression toward average performance. All that new money coming into the fund forces changes in the investment strategy. Portfolio managers can be forced to buy stocks that are either overpriced or lower quality. Consequently, performance often suffers.

WHAT ABOUT STARS?

A lot of credence is given to Chicago's Morningstar four- and five-star rating system, even though it was never intended to be a predictive rating system. The star system is a gauge of how much a fund earned in relation to risk and as compared with similar funds. Again, it is always based on past performance.

According to an article appearing in *The Boston Globe* on April 4, 1999, more than 90 percent of all new mutual fund investments go into funds that have four- and five-star ratings.[1] In the years 1995, 1996, and 1997, the funds with four stars had the strongest "aggregate" performance, although many were outperformed by three-star issues. On average, three-star funds did better than five-star funds.

IT DOESN'T MEAN THEY'RE BAD

Actually, this is not a criticism of Morningstar or of its star system. Mutual funds have a tendency to run hot and cold on performance.

---

1. Charles A. Jaffe, "If You're Buying a High-Flying Fund, You May Already Be a Loser,"
   The Boston Globe, April 4, 1999.

That's partly why they should always be long-term investments. It's the growth over 5, 10, and 20 years that will help the investor reach his or her investment objective. The problem is that it's too easy to get overexcited about top performance and forget objectives, strategy, and risk factors.

PERFORMANCE CONSISTENCY

Rather than trying to chase the performance of top funds, look for funds in line with an established, specific objective. Check the performance consistency year after year. Find the fund that has an acceptable and consistent performance record. Although it's OK to compare funds, just remember that things change. What happened last year could be completely different from what happens this year or next year.

CHAPTER 43

The First Month Determines the Year

In the stock market, some say the first 6 days determine what will happen by the end of the year. The idea of 6 days may go back a few years to when the stock exchanges were open on Saturdays. Others say the first week of the year is the determiner. Still others believe the month of January is the great market forecaster. As goes January, so goes the year.

PICK AN INDEX

Some people measure the year using the Standard & Poor's 500 Index, and others use the Dow Industrial Average. To analyze this beginning-of-the-year phenomenon, we will look at both the S&P 500 Index (SPX) and the Dow Industrial Average (INDU).

The 1-Month Picture

How did the Standard & Poor's 500 Index do in the first month? Quite well! (See Table 43-1.) Wrong only twice in nine years (minor differences) is not a bad record, even for this modest sampling. Additionally, the January forecaster for the S&P 500 Index correctly predicted 1990 as a down year. The S&P 500 Index had an up first month for 1994 (up 15.16), but the index closed the year actually down 7.18 points. This is a minor difference.

TABLE 43-1

The First Month: Standard & Poor's 500 Index

Date	SPX	January ±	Year ±
12/29/89	353.40		
1/31/90	329.08	−24.32	
12/31/90	330.22		−23.18
1/31/91	343.93	13.71	
12/31/91	417.09		86.87
1/31/92	408.79	−8.3	
12/31/92	435.71		**18.62**
1/29/93	438.78	3.07	
12/31/93	466.45		30.74
1/31/94	481.61	15.16	
12/30/94	459.27		**−7.18**
1/31/95	470.42	11.15	
12/29/95	615.93		156.66
1/31/96	636.02	20.09	
12/31/96	740.74		124.81
1/31/97	786.16	45.42	
12/31/97	970.43		229.69
1/30/98	980.28	9.85	
12/31/98	1,229.23		258.80
1/29/99	1,279.64	50.41	

According to the January forecast with the Standard & Poor's 500 Index, 1999 should be an up year. It will be interesting to see the result.

And now for the Dow. As you can see from Table 43-2, the Dow Industrial Average got them all correct except for 1998, where the Dow Industrials were down −1.75 at the end of January, but up 1,273.18 points for the year. The only down year was 1990. January was down 162.66 points for the month, and the year closed less than that, at a negative 119.54 points.

Note that 1994, a crazy year, had January up 224.27, but the year ended up only 80.35, and that was thanks to a Santa Claus rally. There doesn't seem to be any consistent relationship between amounts. The January 1995 increase was only 9.42 points, but the Dow Industrial Average finished the year up 1,282.68 points.

A LARGER SAMPLING OF THE "JANUARY BAROMETER"

If you want to read more about the "January barometer," check out *Stock Trader's Almanac*. In this annual book, the noted statistician Yale Hirsch includes no fewer than four interesting sections on the subject:

> "The Incredible January Barometer—Only Three Significant Errors in 48 Years"

TABLE 43-2

The First Month: Dow Industrial Average

Date	INDU	January	Year
12/29/89	2,753.20		
1/31/90	2,590.54	−162.66	
12/31/90	2,633.66		−119.54
1/31/91	2,736.39	102.73	
12/31/91	3,168.83		535.17
1/31/92	3,223.39	54.56	
12/31/92	3,301.11		132.28
1/29/93	3,310.03	8.92	
12/31/93	3,754.09		452.98
1/31/94	3,978.36	224.27	
12/30/94	3,834.44		80.35
1/31/95	3,843.86	9.42	
12/29/95	5,117.12		1,282.68
1/31/96	5,395.30	278.18	
12/31/96	6,448.27		1,331.15
1/31/97	6,813.09	364.82	
12/31/97	7,908.25		1,459.98
1/30/98	7,906.50	−1.75	
12/31/98	9,181.43		**1,273.18**
1/29/99	9,358.93	177.50	

"January Barometer in Graphic Form"

"January's First Five Days: An Early Warning System"

"1933 Lame Duck Amendment Reason January Barometer Works"[1]

Mr. Hirsch has spent many years analyzing stock market statistics and drawing conclusions from trading patterns that developed. His *Almanac* has been published for the past 31 years.

CHANGE, THE ONLY CERTAINTY

The investor must always remember that the stock market or individual stock prices do not have to follow set patterns or traditional trends. Indicators don't predict; rather they are an implication of what might happen. One thing certain is that trading in the stock market is based on anticipation. It is the anticipation of higher earnings and prices that drives the market up and the anticipation of lower earnings or prices that drives it down. The anticipation factor is not likely to go away. It is an essential part of a public securities market that is freely traded, open, fair, and orderly.

---

1. Information on *The 1999 Stock Trader's Almanac* can be found on the Internet at http://www.hirschorganization.com/almanac.htm.

CHAPTER 44

Size Matters

What's the big deal about size? Isn't a supergiant mutual fund better than a pittance couple-of-hundred-million-dollar fund? If the fund gets into trouble, can't the big fund end up in better shape? In 1987, while fund manager Peter Lynch was kissing the Blarney Stone on his first real vacation in well over a decade, Fidelity Magellan was losing billions of dollars. The fund survived that October 1987 crash, although if it had been only a $3 billion fund it would have been out of business. Mr. Lynch would have been in the unemployment line. So what's all this about funds closing because they're too big?

BIG AND BEAUTIFUL

It's not so much that they're just big, but rather that they're big and beautiful. Imagine for a moment that you're the portfolio manager of a $5 billion aggressive growth fund, investing in small and mid-sized companies. Some new MBA from a prestigious school sells an article to a large-circulation magazine, naming your fund as one of the most promising of its peers. The following week you have another hundred million to invest.

NO MORE THAN 5 PERCENT

The problem is that you can't own more than 5 percent of any one company without running into regulatory reporting requirements

with the SEC. You can't afford that—too much time involved. So
you now have to find new companies. But these have to be companies that won't tarnish your great record. You're too smart to
lower your standards, so the only thing left is to raise them. You
can only look to better and bigger companies and meanwhile put
the money in short-term Treasuries while you figure out a new
strategy. In the meantime, the market goes crazy, down 200 points
on the Dow one day, then up 250 points the next. You know the
volatility will continue for a few days and the portfolio has more
than a few vulnerable spots. After a couple of weeks the market
settles down and becomes flat to slightly up.

Meanwhile a second hundred million dollars enters the cash
coffer. The problem has now doubled in size. If enough time has
passed, all that cash will start to make the fund look bad. You start
buying; the market gains strength; you keep buying stock. You are
now buying stock at the top, the high for the year for some of the
companies. The portfolio is falling victim to "market-cap creep,"
buying larger and larger companies at rising prices, but you have
no choice. The money has to be invested and you keep buying.

SORCERER'S APPRENTICE

If the new stock is well selected and the market continues to be
strong, your fund will continue to be a top performer, and that in
turn will attract more cash, which will need to be invested. Like the
sorcerer's apprentice, it's just too much of a good thing. Eventually,
something's got to give. Either the fund will have to be closed to
new investors, the market cap will continue to creep upward, or
performance will begin to suffer.

Obviously, mutual fund companies are not fond of closing
funds. By closing, they sacrifice the revenue from the additional
management fees. Nevertheless, they don't want a fund to become
a poor performer, so they eventually close to new investors. Later,
when things settle down, some funds will reopen.

SMALL-COMPANY FUND

Being too big is a special problem for mutual funds investing in
smaller companies. With too much cash, they eventually have to

lower standards or buy larger companies. Either choice can negatively impact performance. When small-cap companies slide out of favor (as in the late 1990s), the problem becomes even greater. Senior editor at *Money* magazine, Walter Updegrave, puts it this way:

> I'd also be wary of buying a small-company fund once its assets go very far over the $500 million mark. Why? Because I would be concerned that in order to invest the fund's assets, the manager might buy larger companies than he or she ordinarily would.[1]

At the very least, an investor should check the fund's portfolio to see if it has become subject to market-cap creep over the past few years.

CONCERN, NOT OBSESSION

It's prudent to have some concern about size, although it is just one factor of many that the investor needs to be aware of when selecting a mutual fund. "Too big" can have advantages with a large-capitalization fund, but it is a disadvantage for a fund investing in medium- and small-sized companies.

---

1. Walter Updegrave, *How to Pick Winning Funds,* Warner, 1996.

Closed-End Funds
Trade like Stocks

Closed-end funds can be called tradable mutual funds. A closed-end fund (CEF) is a basket or group of stocks put together in funds. The funds trade on a stock exchange just like common stock. Order qualifiers (limit, stop, and others) can be used, and the trade is executed when it is possible to do so, not only at the end of the day. Some CEFs are less liquid (trade less frequently) than stocks, and a limit order (set price) rather than a market order (best available price) is often the better route.

FIXED NUMBER OF SHARES

An open-ended mutual fund issues new shares of the fund to every new investor. A closed-end fund has a set number of shares. In order for an investor to buy shares, someone has to be selling shares. That's why they trade on a stock exchange.

BUY SHARES THROUGH A BROKER

To buy and sell shares of a CEF, you need to place orders through a stockbroker, who sends your order to the stock exchange. Brokers charge a fee or commission. It will be either a percentage of the transaction or a flat-rate fee. There are now three types of stockbrokers: full service, discount, and deep discount. A full-service broker provides research and information, including investment advice specific to your needs.

SETTING UP AN ACCOUNT

When a broker is selected, it will be necessary to set up a cash account and possibly a margin account. In a cash account, all securities purchased are fully paid by the settlement date, normally on the trade date plus three business days (T+3). A margin account allows the investor to borrow against fully paid securities to buy additional securities. Margin accounts are also used for selling short (selling securities before buying them) and trading options. The use of margin accounts has extra risk and should be studied as a separate subject. Most brokers can send out an information booklet to individual investors on margin accounts and on trading options.

ROUND LOTS

Like common stocks, closed-end funds are normally traded in round lots of 100 shares or multiples of 100 (200, 300, etc.). Trading in fewer than 100 shares is an odd-lot transaction, and it is subject to an additional fee.

TRACKING YOUR CEFS

The market price of the CEF is printed in many newspapers under the stock listings of the exchange on which the CEF trades. For example, if the CEF is XYZ Fund and trades on the New York Stock Exchange, the price information will be found in the letter X stock listings for NYSE. The information gives the 52-week high and low, the volume traded, the high, low, and closing price, the price change, and other information such as the dividend yield, ex-dividend, etc.

NAV

The net asset value of the closed-end fund is published weekly in many newspapers including Monday's *Wall Street Journal* and

Barron's and Saturday's *New York Times* under the section "Publicly Traded Funds" or "Closed-End Funds." Normally, the NAV, the market price, the amount of discount or premium, and the 52-week change is shown. The same information is readily available from a variety of Internet sources.

PREMIUM OR DISCOUNT TO NAV

Earlier in this chapter, it was stated that closed-end funds trade like common stocks on a stock exchange. The most important difference between the two is that the CEF will trade at a discount (less than) or premium (more than) to its net asset value. The net asset value of the CEF is the total market value of the securities in the fund less any management fees or expenses.

Name	NAV	Market Price	Premium*	Discount*
XYZ Fund	$10.00	$12.00	20%	
XYZ Fund	$10.00	$8.00		20%

*Premium or discount = (market price − NAV) / NAV

WIDE DISCOUNT

Investors who trade closed-end funds track the premium/discount situation. If a discount becomes wider than usual, it is similar to a stock being undervalued and can become a buy signal. There is risk involved, because the wider discount usually means investors are selling and the price is declining. The discount is believed by many to be caused by a combination of relatively illiquid trading and the portfolio management fees charged by the funds. Illiquid trading is caused by periods of a lack of investor interest. The lack of interest might cause the price to decline, but not necessarily. Many times shareholders will hold their shares, waiting for investor interest to return.

COUNTRY FUNDS

In the early part of the 1990s, "country funds" (Germany Fund, Mexico Fund, Emerging Market Fund, etc.) were highly popular.

Many of them lost their popularity in the sell-off of 1994 and have remained out of favor. During this time several of the countries involved with closed-end funds had economic difficulties.

SPECULATIVE PORTFOLIOS

There are closed-end funds other than just country funds. Some funds invest in private placements, provide venture capital, or invest in companies under bankruptcy reorganization. A valuation of these investments is difficult. The investments are usually very speculative, with investments in growth capital, leveraged buy-outs, or recapitalization of existing companies. Risk is moderated by incorporating the risky investments in the structure of a fund. Some ventures will fail, but others might succeed. They tend to trade at a discount.

MAIN ADVANTAGE

The main advantage of closed-end funds is that they provide access to interested investors. Private placements normally have significant net worth requirements, which could involve too much money for many individuals. Some countries have restrictions on foreigners owning their companies' stock. The CEF enables the investor to make these investments.

CHAPTER 46

Compare the Fund Features

For many years, mutual fund companies have been presenting the features and benefits of investing in their funds. The ability to buy partial shares, buy no-loads, do automated buying or selling, reinvest dividends and capital gains, and make exchanges from one fund to another (in the same fund family) are just some of the many advantages of buying mutual funds. The features are generally not available if one owns just the individual stock. They are only available through mutual funds. Although features can be slightly different from one fund family to the next, they tend to be similar. Here is a review of some mutual fund features.

AUTOMATIC BUYING

Although any required initial minimum must be met, once an account is established, the investor can set up a plan to have the mutual fund automatically pull a set amount of money from his or her personal bank account to purchase stock in the fund. Doing this automatically, on, say, a monthly basis, establishes a dollar cost averaging system of mutual fund purchase. The strategy results in buying more shares when prices are lower and fewer shares when prices are higher, effectively lowering the average cost.

DIVIDEND REINVESTMENT

The automatic reinvestment of dividends and capital gains paid by the fund also has an effect similar to dollar cost averaging. Many load funds do dividend and capital gain reinvestment without charging the load for the new purchases.

AUTOMATIC WITHDRAWAL

The fund will send you a check on a regular basis. Shares are sold and a check can be sent, usually as often as once a month. Most funds allow the investor to set the schedule and frequency of payment, but may require the investor to maintain a minimum dollar value amount in the account. It is possibly to deplete the assets in the account using an automatic withdrawal program. That's why funds set a minimum balance. The minimum is often $10,000.

TELEPHONE REDEMPTION

Telephone redemptions can have the proceeds sent directly to the investor's bank account.

WIRE REDEMPTION

For a nominal fee (often $5) proceeds can be wired to the investor's personal bank account and be available for use as soon as they arrive.

REDEMPTION SENT TO BANK

Redemptions can be sent to the investor's bank account and be available for use in just a few days. A confirmation of the transfer of funds is sent to the investor.

PAYROLL DEDUCTIONS

Many firms have payroll deduction programs where a designated amount is sent directly to the mutual fund.

AUTOMATIC DIVIDEND TRANSFER

Investors in one fund can have dividends and distributions reinvested into another fund within the same mutual fund family. This transfer of dividends is somewhat of an asset allocation strategy.

EXCHANGE PRIVILEGES

Investors can move assets from one mutual fund to another in the same fund family. There may be some restrictions about which funds are available, as well as possible minimum initial investment requirements. Some funds charge a small fee, and others limit the number of exchanges that can be made in a year.

CHECKING ACCOUNT PRIVILEGES

Many mutual funds now attach checking accounts to some of their funds. Often the checking account is attached to a money market account. Learn the specific details of any attached checking account. Some have fees and minimums.

TELEPHONE OR ONLINE ARRANGEMENTS

Probably all mutual fund companies can implement your directives by telephone. It's a fast, easy way to move your money around as necessary. More and more fund companies are setting up home pages on the Internet. The fund sites provide valuable current information about their fund families, and many allow the investors to view their personal accounts as well as issue instructions.

CHAPTER 47

Index Funds Follow
the Market

Always keep in mind that volatility means prices move up and prices move down. If prices move up, it's usually acceptable to most investors. It's the down that they have trouble with, the price decline. The way money flows into an advancing market, you'd swear the investors don't even want to see lower prices.

However, markets fluctuate. They change daily, as anticipation changes. One day earnings reports are positive and inflation prospects are low. The next day a large company announces lower earnings and the market tanks. Interest rates rise, or a deteriorating economic situation in one country has global implications. The market slips into a bearish decline, and investors worry about the safety of their mutual funds.

THREE PERFORMANCE CHOICES

Essentially, performance can be divided into three broad performance strategies, with different levels of risk:

Performance Strategy	Risk Acceptance
Beat the market	Greater risk
Equal the market	Equal risk
Be lower than the market	Lower risk

Index funds fall in the middle, striving to equal the market to which they are indexed. One of the big advantages of having a mutual fund tied to an index is the low management expense. There is little to manage; therefore expenses should be low.

NOBEL BEGINNINGS

The concept of indexing originated in the mid-1970s with Paul Samuelson, a Nobel laureate economist. Samuelson observed that whereas many stock pickers try to beat the market average, only a small number succeed. As it turns out, the performance of two-thirds to three-fourths of all mutual funds trails the market average, as compared with the S&P 500 Index.

Samuelson discovered some good reasons for the failure to beat the market average. The cost of trading, administration, and other fees means that a mutual fund manager must beat the market by 2 percentage points to come out even after expenses. When the market goes up 12 percent, the manager has to make 14 percent to do better.

Indexing had the intent of minimizing trading. In turn it could virtually eliminate management fees and reduce fund management costs. A portfolio of stocks could be assembled to match the index. The investor matched market performance at a low cost. What could be better? If you want to match index performance, then match the stocks in the index. The only unusual part of the idea is that it took a Nobel laureate, an economist, to come up with it.

CAN THEY DO IT?

According to John Bogle, the chairman and founder of the Vanguard Group, an index fund with an adequately low management fee can match the S&P 500 Index by 99 percent. Additionally, the index fund remains virtually fully invested at all times. It needs a small amount of cash for normal redemptions, but the rest stays in the stock market. No need to hold cash for technical analysis or market timing strategies. No headaches, as the fund does what the market does.

SO WHERE'S THE PROBLEM?

There is always a problem when it comes to investing strategies. With index funds it's when the market turns and heads south.

Fully managed portfolios are quick to point out that they can take some protective measures to soften the blow of a declining stock market, although some do decidedly better than others. Unmanaged index funds remain fully invested and are hit as hard as the declining market. As they encounter shareholder redemptions from nervous investors and sell accordingly, the market tanks deeper.

> In the seven year period from 1977 to 1983, the index (S&P 500) beat managers a mere 26% of the time; similarly, in the three year period from 1991 to 1993, that figure is just 44%. Exceptional long-term results depend on the freedom to act on cyclical changes.[1]

The point that Doug Fabian, the author of the quote, is making is that funds with active portfolios have the freedom to act on cyclical changes, but index funds do not. Managers should be able to take some protective measures in declining markets. How well they do depends on the individual fund strategy and the portfolio management.

MANY TO CHOOSE FROM

If an investor wants an index fund, there are now a number from which to choose. Morningstar notes nearly 250 index funds from a variety of mutual fund companies. Whereas the most popular are the S&P 500 and the Wilshire 5000, there are a variety of other options. The ASM Index 30 (ASMUX) follows the Dow Industrials. Bridgeway has superlarge or small-company indexes. Wilshire has eight funds, including the Wilshire Target Large Company Value (DTLVX) and the Wilshire Target Small Company Growth (DTSGX). And one of the pioneers of index funds, Vanguard, now has 25 different index funds.

A recent addition to the index arena has been Internet index funds. *Inter@ctive Week* magazine's 50-company Internet index is popular and widely cited as a web stock index since its beginning in 1995. Index firms include web content firms, service providers, and utilities, and also Internet basic builders such as Adobe, Sun

---

1. Doug Fabian, "Blowing the Whistle on Index Funds," Mutual Funds Interactive, August 1998, http://www.fundsinteractive.com/expert/expfb0898.html.

Microsystems, Qualcomm, and 3Com. The index has more than doubled, from 300 to 650, over the last year (1998–1999).

Mecklermedia's ISDEX index is a comprehensive list of Internet firms. It started up in April 1996, including e-tailers, ISPs, Internet software makers, web portals, and online brokers. From its benchmark of 100 on December 31, 1996, the index has grown to over 370 in just under 3 years.[2]

INDEX FUND GROWTH

index funds have experienced rapid growth, more than twice that of the mutual fund industry. In 1998 index funds set a record, gathering $42 billion, bringing total assets to more than $250 billion. The Standard & Poor's 500 Index holds about 71 percent of all index fund assets and had 60 percent of the 1998 record.[3]

ENHANCED INDEX FUNDS

Although many index funds proclaim their "enhancements," only a few are actually enhanced index funds. Index funds are essentially passively managed as opposed to actively managed. Periodic changes are made in the portfolio as the indexes are changed. Changes occur because some companies are acquired, while others no longer meet the index criteria for inclusion. This is passive management. Active management is changing the portfolio to take advantage of market conditions for the highest possible return. The enhanced index fund is a combination of the two management styles.

ENHANCEMENT METHODS

When considering an enhanced index fund, at least learn and understand the methods of enhancement used. They are usually

---

2. Borzou Daragahi, "Index Information from Web Stock Indexmania," *Virtual Investor,* money.com, February 25, 1999.

   http://www.pathfinder.com/money/virtual/archive/990225.html.

3. Data and fund information from "Index Fund Initiative Paradox," Mutual Fund Café, Financial Research Corporation, April 5, 1999.

complicated, but will provide some insight into risk and potential reward.

Some common methods of enhancement are (from the Ibbotson study):

1. *Derivatives.*   Using futures and options as well as margin leverage.
2. *Security-level techniques.*   Capitalizing on perceived mispricings of securities. This method is further divided into:
   a. *Security-level optimization*
      Overweight the undervalued and underweight the overvalued.
      Mean variance—setting a mean and constraining stock impact.
      Sector specialists—an equal weighting of sectors and sector purity.
   b. *Sector/style optimization.*   The manager overweights or underweights sectors, industries, styles that are undervalued or overvalued.
   c. *Hybrid.*   The hybrid uses both individual company and sector/style factors.

WHERE'S THE INDEX?

It's easy to see from this brief description that one might begin to wonder if enhanced index funds ever actually invest in the index they intend to enhance. It's almost as if they were to buy the top-performing stock in any given index and then trade options and futures. It might work, but it might not. Looking at it from the other perspective, if the managers are careful and choose a conservative approach, there isn't much enhancement. Why not select a good growth fund instead?

TAXES

Another problem with the enhanced index fund is the frequent trading that can occur. When trades result in capital distributions to the investor, it becomes a taxable event. Many funds, including regular index funds, avoid such events.

INDEX OR NO INDEX

The main point is how index funds fit into the investor's objective. They can certainly be considered and usually have an additional advantage of low expense. However, they should not be added to the portfolio because they were hot last year or this year. Also, because index funds tend to be overweighted in larger-cap funds, an investor should have more diversification than to be in just one index fund.

CHAPTER 48

Invest in Tax-Free Funds

Tax-exempt municipal bonds (munis) are debt obligations issued by municipalities, states, cities, counties, and other governmental entities. The purpose of the bonds is to raise money for building schools, highways, hospitals, and sewer systems, as well as many other projects for the public good. While there are several types of investments that provide an investor with tax-exempt income, they all utilize municipal bonds as their source.

NO TAX

Interest income on most municipal bonds is exempt from federal and, in some cases, state and local income taxes for those living in the state of issue. The tax exemption enables local and state governments to borrow money at lower interest costs than corporations or even the federal government. The lower cost of borrowing obviously saves money for state and local governments. The tax-exempt status[1] also makes the bonds highly attractive to investors.

---

1. For some tax-exempt municipal bonds, some investors' income may be subject to the federal alternative minimum tax.

TAXABLE EQUIVALENT YIELD

One way to look at tax-free bonds and non-tax-free bonds is to calculate the *taxable equivalent yield*. The taxable equivalent yield is the interest a taxable bond would have to pay to equal the return on a tax-free bond. Anything larger than the yield indicates the taxable bond or fund is a better deal. A lesser amount indicates the tax-free bond is more equitable.

The taxable equivalent yield is:

Tax-free yield, stated as a decimal (divide the percent by 100)
Divided by 1.0 minus the investor's tax bracket, stated as a decimal (divide % by 100)
Equals the taxable equivalent yield

For example, assume that the investor is considering a 6 percent municipal bond fund and that the investor is in the 28 percent highest tax bracket:

$$6\% \text{ divided by } 100 = 0.06$$
$$28\% \text{ divided by } 100 = 0.28$$
$$1.0 - 0.28 = 0.72$$
$$0.06 \text{ divided by } 0.72 = 8.33\% \quad \text{(taxable equivalent yield)}$$

A taxable bond or fund would have to pay an investor in the 28 percent tax bracket 8.33 percent to equal the return on a tax-free bond. Anything higher than 8.33 percent on a taxable corporate would make it the higher-yielding bond.

UNDERSTANDING YIELDS

Like other types of bonds, munis have current yield and yield to maturity. Current yield is the annual return on the dollar amount paid for a bond (essentially coupon dollar amount divided by current price).

Yield to maturity is the return received by holding a bond until it matures. The calculation includes price, coupon, and time as factors. It can provide a quick comparison of one bond to another.

When the price of a tax-exempt bond increases above its face value, it sells at a premium. When the bond sells below face value, it sells at a discount. Price changes for bonds are determined by changes in interest rates.

DIFFERS WITH BOND FUNDS

With a muni bond mutual fund, changes in interest rates affect the net asset value. If interest rates rise, the NAV drops, but if interest rates go lower, the NAV increases. The movement of interest rates is especially important when looking at a bond fund's total return (price increase plus dividends). Interest rates have dropped significantly lower since 1989 to 1999. Although they could go lower yet, it would be impossible for a repeat of the past decade. Interest rates cannot go to zero or below, even with a total financial collapse. On March 31, 1989, the 30-year U.S. Treasury bond had a yield of 9.11 percent. On the same day of 1999 that yield had fallen to 5.63 percent, down 3.48 percent for the decade. If it fell the same amount in the next decade, the 30-year Treasury yield would be 2.15 percent.

HOW SAFE ARE MUNICIPAL BONDS?

The primary concern with bonds should be the issuer's ability to pay interest and return the principal at maturity. Most issuers of municipal bonds have excellent records of meeting payments.

Details of the financial condition can be examined in either official statements or offering circulars available from banks, brokerage firms, or a library of official statements.

MUNIS HAVE BOND RATINGS

Munis also have credit ratings. Many are graded by agencies such as Moody's Investors Service, Standard & Poor's Corporation, and Fitch Investors Service, Inc. Additionally, some banks and brokerage firms have research departments to analyze muni bonds.

Bond credit ratings are important. They reflect a professional assessment of the issuer's ability to pay interest and return the bond's face value at maturity.

Bonds rated BBB, BAA, or better by Standard & Poor's and Fitch, or Moody's, respectively, are generally considered investment grade, suitable for preservation of investment capital. Obviously, more risk-aversive investors can raise that to say AA or better, and speculative investors can lower the standard for higher yields.

Look at the information to see how the bond portfolio is spread through the various risk categories. Muni funds tend to buy muni bonds that are investment grade or better. The highest credit rating on bonds is AAA.

MARKET RISK

While the coupon rate cannot be changed during the existence of a bond (except for a variable-rate security), the market price changes as market conditions change. If munis are sold before reaching maturity, they receive the current market price. If the bonds were purchased at face value (par) and interest rates have risen, the selling price will bring less than face value. If interest rates are lower, the price will be higher than face value.

Mutual funds for munis adjust the net asset value according to the price of the bonds in the portfolio.

SPECIAL FEATURES

Insured Municipal Bonds

Some municipal bond issues are insured to reduce investment risk. If the bonds default, the insurance company guarantees payment of both interest and principal when due. The cost for the insurance comes out of the yield. In other words, insured bonds normally have lower yields than comparable uninsured bonds.

Floating-Rate and Variable-Rate Bonds

The interest payment from the bond changes as interest rates change. The rate is generally based on U.S. Treasury yields or on some other basic index.

Zero-Coupon Muni Bonds

Like other zeros, munis are issued at a deep discount from their face value at maturity. They do not pay out interest. Instead the interest compounds at the stated interest rate. The investor receives one payment, containing principal and interest, at maturity. Zeros are especially well suited to investors who do not need the current cash flow from investments.

TYPES OF MUNICIPAL BONDS

Municipal securities have short- and long-term issues. Short-term bonds, often called notes, usually mature in a year or less. Short-term notes are used to raise money in anticipation of future revenues, such as taxes, state or federal aid payments, or bond proceeds. The notes are also issued to meet unanticipated deficits or raise cash for projects temporarily until longer bond financing can be arranged. Short-term notes pay interest on maturity. Long-term bonds normally have maturities of more than a year (2 to 30 years). Bonds are usually sold to finance capital projects over the longer term. They normally pay interest every 6 months. The basic types of municipal securities are general obligation bonds and revenue bonds.

General Obligation Bonds (GO Bonds)

The payment of principal and interest is secured by the full faith and credit of the issuer. General obligation bonds are supported by the issuer's ability to tax.

Revenue Bonds (Rev Bonds)

The payment of principal and interest is secured by the revenues earned by the facility that was constructed using the money from the bond issue. Public-use projects like highways, bridges, airports, commercial boat landings, water and sewage treatment facilities, hospitals, and housing for the poor are constructed with the funds from municipal revenue bonds. Revenue bonds normally do not depend on the taxing ability of a municipality. Therefore they can have some higher risk in certain situations. The revenue-generating facility has to earn enough income to meet the interest and principal payments.

MINIMUM INVESTMENT

Most tax-exempt municipal bonds are issued in denominations of $5,000 or integral multiples of $5,000. Most notes are also available with a minimum denomination of $5,000.

Bond mutual funds and unit trusts can have different minimum requirements. Some are $10,000 for the initial investment and $1,000 for additional investments. Others have a minimum of $1,000 initially.

SET AN OBJECTIVE AND SEARCH

First a general tax-exempt income objective can be established, with other specifications (yield, ratings, fund size, management, and risk) added when information is gathered. Sales charges and fees can be more important to an income objective, because they are less likely to be absorbed with better performance.

When a fund is purchased, the current yield on those shares stays the same as long as the dividend doesn't change. When the dividend goes up, the yield rises also. If the dividend decreases, the yield also decreases. Yield is the current dividend dollar amount divided by the price paid, multiplied by 100. When the investor buys additional shares, those shares could have a different yield than the original shares.

PART OF A PORTFOLIO

Tax-exempt municipal bond funds can be an important part of an investor's portfolio. Obviously, the tax exemption is a large benefit to many, but also muni bonds are important to the communities' development. It's a good way of investing in one's home state, to help out and be paid interest. The funds for the bonds often do much to improve the quality of life for everyone living in the state.

CHAPTER 49

Know the Investment Theme

Themes for investing come in a variety of flavors. Some are quite general, like global investing or a theme of low interest rates and a strong economy. Others are fairly specific, such as Internet stock investing, or even more specific, like Internet service providers (ISP).

THEME AS AN INVESTMENT STRATEGY

William J. Newman, the portfolio manager of Phoenix, a fund based in Enfield, Connecticut, is credited with starting the idea of theme investing. He began the strategy back in the early 1980s, and it has become a commonly used term for describing new growth areas.

The idea is to separate the solid growth ideas from the short-lived fads and invest early in the development cycle. Pet rocks and Cabbage Patch dolls were fads, but Internet development has growth potential. Rollerblading was not a fad, but apparently Newman's analysis came up with too much manufacturing competition.

Bill Newman identified four stages that a theme goes through: discovery, conviction, exploitation, and saturation.

Discovery. At this stage, trends are noticed and talked about.

Conviction.   Individual investors begin to buy the stocks.

Exploitation.   Big investors and institutional investors buy the stock.

Saturation.   Sales and earnings start to slow.

BECOMING INVOLVED

It's obvious that the best time to find an investment theme is at the discovery stage (or sooner). The problem is that mutual funds have probably not become involved at this stage. Funds will often not enter a theme until the exploitation stage. Then they hop on the bandwagon to build a fund. This action adds to the fast growth of the exploitation, pushing prices to a higher peak.

WHEN IT'S OVER

Although the quick speculative hit is over when exploitation reaches a peak and saturation takes over, prices settle down and "normal" growth follows. If the themes are sound and not just passing fads, they may never be over.

SOME ONGOING THEMES

Health care is still growing and will last because it's connected with the "graying of America" theme. It's a wide-ranging theme from hospitals to nursing homes, long-term care, HMOs, medical technology, drugs, medical devices, and biotechnology. The Internet is in an exploitation stage that will push the limits, but it is likely to stay with us as an extension of the television, computers, and technology theme. The Internet could change the demographics of office work. An employer in Chicago can hire experts from around the world, and they come to work via the Internet.

GEOGRAPHIC THEME

An example of a fund family that is invested in growth companies located in specific geographic areas is Aquila. The Aquila Rocky

Mountain Equity Fund limits itself to Colorado, Arizona, Idaho, Montana, Nevada, New Mexico, Utah, and Wyoming. It buys into companies based in those states or doing at least half their business there. A second fund, Aquila Cascadia Equity Fund, represents the Northwest: Oregon, Washington, Alaska, and Hawaii, plus Idaho, Utah, and Nevada, which are also in the Rocky Mountain Equity Fund.

> Aquila Rocky Mountain invests in the highest growth area of the U.S. A decade ago Utah was home to a handful of high tech companies. Now, there are about 150 software firms in the new Silicon Strip between Provo and Salt Lake City.[1]

SOUNDS EXCITING

Themes often sound exciting, especially when they reach the point of being actively promoted. Investors who find the ideas interesting need to investigate further to see if the funds are well established and at a fair cost. Of course, that's once the investor decides the fund fits the investor's objective and risk tolerance level.

OTHER THEMES

There are several different investing themes around. Some are successful, and others fade away. There are socially responsible investing funds, environmental issues funds, specialty funds for women (e.g., The Woman's Equity Fund), and athletics funds (e.g., Sportsfund), to name a few. On a lighter side, the Gabelli Global Interactive Couch Potato Fund invests in companies related to home entertainment, publishing, and media stocks. With a little searching an investor can find funds based on a variety of themes. The trick is to pick the next "hot" investment theme and get in on the action early enough to ride the wave.

---

1. John Tompkins, Portfolio "Theme Funds," November 15, 1996. John Tompkins is a New York–based financial analyst, adviser, and award-winning author of numerous financial books. He provides insight into mutual funds. http://talks.com/library/jt111596.html.

ANALYSIS

The analysis for theme funds should be like that for any mutual fund. Get the prospectus and learn about the fund. Look at the fund's objective and strategy. Growth figures can give some idea of the fund's current theme stage. The main risks are that the theme may already have had its day or might never become hot.

DIVERSIFICATION

If the theme is too narrow, there could be a diversification problem. There might not be enough companies around to spread the risk. In the early days, the Internet had a similar problem. As the Internet grew and became popular, the diversification improved. Diversification should be part of the risk analysis of theme investing.

CHAPTER 50

Consider a Wrap as a Fund Alternative

Want to know some alternatives to mutual fund investing? You can do the analysis and buy the stock yourself. The analysis part is the most important and the most difficult. You can hire an investment adviser to sell you mutual funds that you could have found with a couple hours of searching. Or when your net worth is large enough, you can consider doing a wrap account.

WHAT IS A WRAP?

A wrap account is a fee-based investment program that can be arranged with your brokerage firm. The program can have different names depending on the marketing approach of the brokerage firm. There are two types of wrap accounts: a traditional wrap account and a mutual fund wrap account.

Traditional Wrap

The traditional wrap offers several brokerage services for one fee, normally based on a percentage of the value of the investment portfolio. Fees are generally 1 to 3 percent and require a minimum investment of $100,000 to $200,000 in the account. The fee is for commissions and other transaction costs, as well as professional planning fees.

Mutual Fund Wrap

A mutual fund wrap account often has a minimum of $10,000 to $15,000, and the account fees average about 2 percent.

THE GOOD SIDE

Investing has a bit of a high learning curve and takes time. Having a knowledgeable manager handle the details can save that time for other activities. Saving time as well as avoiding headaches like money management is important to many people. It's much easier and less time consuming to sit back and judge the manager's performance.

The money manager has a reason to increase the value of the portfolio—the fee is based on the portfolio's value. It's a strong business incentive to do well.

The investor doesn't have to be concerned with individual commission charges if the account is being excessively turned over.

The portfolio is managed to meet your personal goals and objectives by someone who should know how to do it best.

THE OTHER SIDE

Trust

Obviously, the relationship must be one of trust. The investor must trust the abilities of the portfolio manager. If the money manager decides to do nothing with the account, it is still charged the wrap fee of 2 to 3 percent.

Attention

Investors are led to believe that their investments will receive personal attention from the professional money manager. But does this really happen, or does the individual get lost in a hundred other, perhaps bigger, accounts? Ask how many accounts the manager controls.

Fees

Mutual fund wrap accounts might have layers of fees attached. The investor pays the wrap fee and pays the individual mutual fund fees as well. In fact, there can be as many as five fee layers. There might be an origination fee (possibly 2 percent, effectively a sales charge), a load on the mutual funds, a maintenance fee (could be $^2/_5$ percent), and the management fees for the mutual funds. A fifth can be a "custodial" fee for holding the account at the firm. With some wraps, this can easily add up to a 5 percent annual fee. The biggest problem with high annual fees is 5 or 10 years away, when nothing changes much in the portfolio, but the charges still go against the account.

Limited Selection

The selection of mutual funds may be limited to in-house proprietary funds or possibly just a handful of funds. If the fund selection meets the investor's objective and the specific details are acceptable, this might not be a serious problem.

ALTERNATIVES

Might a selection of three or four carefully chosen mutual funds accomplish a similar or possibly even better goal? How about a growth fund, an income fund, and an index fund, with the assets spread according to what is needed now and in the future?

If an investor lacks knowledge of investing and has neither the desire nor the time to learn, a fee-based adviser can come up with a comprehensive plan. The adviser can either help with the investing or not. Sometimes, a little good planning will be enough to head the investor toward achieving his or her objective.

INDEX

ABOUT THE AUTHOR

Michael D. Sheimo has extensive experience as a registered representative and registered options principal, working as a broker at the full service retail level for Merrill Lynch and Olde Financial Corporation. He is an internationally recognized expert on the Dow Theory and has had books published in India, Malaysia, and Japan. He works as an author and independent business consultant in the Minneapolis area.